Mary Engelbreit

FAN FARE COOKBOOK

120 dessert recipe favorites

Other cookbooks from Mary Engelbreit

Mary Engelbreit's Queen of the Kitchen Cookbook

Mary Engelbreit's Sweet Treats Dessert Cookbook

*Mary Engelbreit's Fan Fare Cookbook:
120 Family Favorite Recipes*

*Mary Engelbreit's Fan Fare Cookbook:
120 Slow Cooker Recipe Favorites*

Mary Engelbreit's

FAN FARE COOKBOOK

120 dessert recipe favorites

Illustrated by
Mary Engelbreit

Recipes by Friends and Fans

**Andrews McMeel
Publishing, LLC**

Kansas City • Sydney • London

Andrews McMeel Publishing, LLC
an Andrews McMeel Universal company
1130 Walnut Street, Kansas City, Missouri 64106

www.andrewsmcmeel.com

13 14 15 16 17 TEN 10 9 8 7 6 5 4 3 2 1

ISBN: 978-1-4494-0060-6

Library of Congress Control Number: 2012951927

® and Mary Engelbreit® are registered trademarks of Mary Engelbreit Enterprises, Inc.
www.maryengelbreit.com

www.andrewsmcmeel.com

Some of the recipes in this book call for prepackaged ingredients. Because package sizes vary by manufacturer, the sizes given are approximates and may vary slightly from brand to brand.

ATTENTION: SCHOOLS AND BUSINESSES
Andrews McMeel books are available at quantity discounts with bulk purchase for educational, business, or sales promotional use. For information, please e-mail the Andrews McMeel Publishing Special Sales Department:
specialsales@amuniversal.com

Contents

If my family had to depend on me for food, they would starve to death in a really cute kitchen.

—Mary Engelbreit

Letter from Mary

It's no secret that I'm not the chef in our family! And even though I do not devote my time to cooking, I still love and appreciate good food.

For this cookbook, I called upon my family, friends, and fans for their favorite desserts, and, boy, did they deliver! Here you'll find recipes for cakes, cheesecakes, pies, tarts, cobblers, crisps, cookies, bars, brownies, candies, breakfast treats, breads, ice creams, puddings, and more. All are decadent and exceptionally delicious!

I hope you enjoy these recipes. Let's get cooking!

Mary

You know you're getting
old when you get that one
candle on the cake. It's like,
"See if you can blow this out."

—Jerry Seinfeld

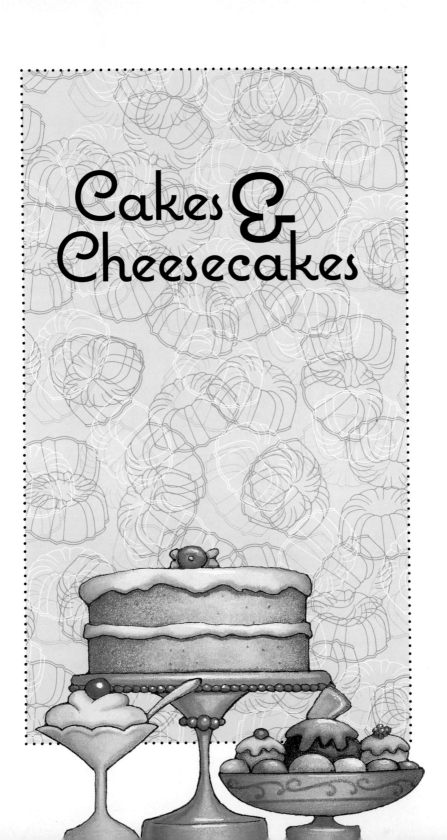

Cakes & Cheesecakes

Ann Rice
Monrovia, California

Mom's Best
White Layer Cake

Makes one 8-inch round cake

1/2 cup shortening
1 1/2 cups sugar
2 eggs
1/2 teaspoon vanilla extract
1/2 teaspoon almond extract
2 cups all-purpose flour
3 1/2 teaspoons
  baking powder
1 cup whole milk

Buttercream Frosting

1/2 cup butter
1 (16-ounce) package
  confectioners' sugar
2 teaspoons vanilla extract
1/4 cup milk (or substitute
  strong instant coffee
  for mocha flavor)

Preheat the oven to 350°F. Grease two 8-inch round cake pans.

In a large bowl with a mixer, cream the shortening and sugar on medium speed. Add the eggs one at a time and blend well after each. Stir in the vanilla and almond extracts. Mix in the flour, baking powder, and milk. Pour the batter into the prepared pans and bake for 30 to 35 minutes, until a toothpick inserted in the center comes out clean. Set the pans on wire racks to cool for 10 minutes, then invert the cakes and cool directly on the racks.

To make the frosting, cream the butter, confectioners' sugar, and vanilla on medium speed. Add the milk slowly until the desired stiff consistency is achieved. After the cake has cooled completely, frost and serve. ■

This is my mother's favorite cake. That in itself makes it extra special to me! It's a classic, just like her. —AR

Annetta Milhon
Grand Island, Nebraska

Tres Leches Cake

Makes one 9-inch cake

5 eggs, separated
3/4 cup plus 1/4 cup
   sugar, divided
1/3 cup milk
1 teaspoon vanilla extract
1 cup all-purpose flour
1 1/2 teaspoons
   baking powder

1 (14-ounce) can sweetened
   condensed milk
1 (12-ounce) can
   evaporated milk
1 3/4 cups plus 1/4
   cup heavy whipping
   cream, divided
10 maraschino cherries

Preheat the oven to 350°F. Butter and flour the bottom of a 9-inch springform pan.

In a medium bowl with a mixer, beat the egg yolks and the 3/4 cup of the sugar until light in color and doubled in volume. Stir in the milk, vanilla, flour, and baking powder.

In a small bowl with the (cleaned and dried) mixer, beat the egg whites on medium speed until soft peaks form. Gradually add the remaining 1/4 cup of sugar. Beat until firm but not dry. Fold the egg whites into the yolk mixture. Pour the batter into the prepared pan. Bake for 45 to 50 minutes, until a toothpick inserted into the center comes out clean. Let cool for 10 minutes, then loosen the edges of the cake with a knife before removing the side of the pan. Let cool completely.

cakes & cheesecakes

{continued}

Place the cake on a deep serving plate. Use a fork to pierce the surface of the cake. In a large bowl, mix together the sweetened condensed milk, evaporated milk, and the 1/4 cup of the whipping cream. Discard 1 cup of the milk mixture. Pour the remaining milk mixture over the cake slowly until it is absorbed.

In a medium bowl, whip the remaining 1 3/4 cups whipping cream until it forms stiff peaks. Frost the cake with the whipped cream and garnish with the cherries. ■

A family from Chile attends our church, and the wife taught me how to make this cake for special birthdays. It is moist and yummy! —AM

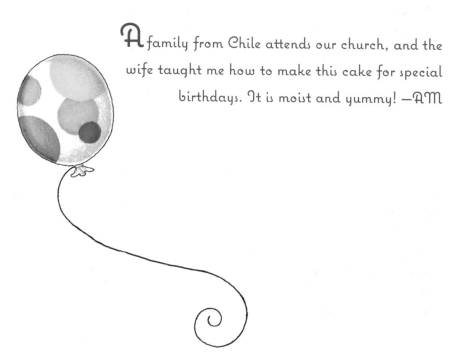

Merrill Hogan-Smith
Yallambie, Australia

Amber Meringue Cake

Makes one 8-inch round cake

1/2 cup butter
1 cup packed light
  brown sugar
1 whole egg
1 egg yolk
1 teaspoon vanilla extract
1 1/2 cups self-rising flour
1/2 cup milk

Filling

1/3 cup butter
1/4 cup packed light
  brown sugar
2 tablespoons cornstarch
Pinch of salt

1 egg yolk
1 cup milk
1/2 teaspoon vanilla extract

Topping

2 egg whites
1/2 cup plus 1 tablespoon
  sugar, divided
1 tablespoon sweetened
  shredded coconut
1 teaspoon ground
  cinnamon
1 tablespoon slivered
  almonds

Preheat the oven to 350°F. Grease two 8-inch round cake pans.

In a large bowl, cream the butter and brown sugar until light and fluffy. Add the egg, egg yolk, and vanilla and beat lightly. Sift the flour and add it to the mixture, alternating with the milk. Mix well. Divide the mixture evenly between the prepared pans. Bake for 20 minutes, or until a toothpick inserted into the center comes out clean. Set the cakes on a wire rack to cool for about 10 minutes, then invert the pans and let the cakes cool directly on the rack. Increase the oven temperature to 400°F.

{continued}

cakes & cheesecakes

5

Amber Meringue Cake
{continued}

While the cakes are cooling, make the filling. In a small saucepan, melt the butter. Add the brown sugar and stir until dissolved. Remove the saucepan from the heat and add the cornstarch and salt. Stir until smooth. Return the saucepan to the heat and simmer gently, stirring constantly. In a small bowl, beat the egg yolk, milk, and vanilla, and then add it to the saucepan, stirring constantly. Simmer for 2 minutes, or until thickened, and then let cool completely.

To make the topping, beat the egg whites in a small bowl until stiff. Add the 1/2 cup of sugar gradually and beat until smooth. In a separate bowl, combine the coconut, the remaining 1 tablespoon of sugar, the cinnamon, and almonds.

Spread the cooled filling between the two cake layers and stack them one on top of the other on a baking sheet or ovenproof plate. Spread the egg white topping on top of the cake, then sprinkle the dry-mixture topping over that. Turn off the oven and place the cake in it for 5 minutes to set the meringue. Remove from the oven and let cool completely before slicing and serving. ■

This delicious cake is a favorite with my sister and me. We used to make it for each other's birthdays. It is best eaten on the day it is made. There is not usually any left over anyway! —MHS

Mary Engelbreit
St. Louis, Missouri

Gooey Butter Cake

Makes one 9 by 13-inch cake

1 (16-ounce) package
  pound cake mix
4 eggs
1/2 cup butter or
  margarine, softened

1 (8-ounce) package
  cream cheese, softened
2 tablespoons vanilla extract
1 (16-ounce) box
  confectioners' sugar

Preheat the oven to 350°F. In a large bowl, blend the cake mix, 2 of the eggs, and the butter. Pour the batter into an ungreased 9 by 13-inch baking dish. In a medium bowl, beat the cream cheese, the remaining 2 eggs, the vanilla, and all but 2 tablespoons of the confectioners' sugar. Pour the mixture on top of the batter. Bake for 15 minutes. Top with the reserved 2 tablespoons of confectioners' sugar and bake for an additional 25 minutes, or until a toothpick inserted in the center comes out clean. ■

This is really a St. Louis tradition, and one of my all-time favorite desserts. Although the customary pies are nice at holiday gatherings, I prefer Gooey Butter Cake instead. —ME

cakes & cheesecakes

Ann Schultz
Springfield, Missouri

Snack Cake Three Ways

Makes one 9 by 13-inch cake

1 (18.5-ounce) box yellow
or white cake mix
1 (4.6-ounce) box instant
chocolate pudding mix
3 eggs
1 teaspoon vanilla extract
1 cup vegetable oil

1 (8-ounce) container
sour cream
1/2 cup water
6 ounces (about 1 cup)
semisweet chocolate chips
Confectioners' sugar,
for garnish

Preheat the oven to 350°F. Grease a 9 by 13-inch baking pan.

In a large bowl, combine the cake mix, pudding mix, eggs, vanilla, oil, sour cream, water, and chocolate chips and stir well. Pour into the prepared pan and bake for 45 minutes, or until a toothpick inserted into the center comes out clean.

Set the pan on a wire rack and let cool completely. Sprinkle the top of the cake with confectioners' sugar just before serving. ∎

Variations

Use red velvet cake mix, cheesecake-flavored pudding, and white chocolate chips.

Use German chocolate cake mix, vanilla pudding, and milk chocolate chips. Add 1/2 cup of sweetened shredded coconut and 1/2 cup of chopped nuts to the batter.

I am a nurse, and I take snacks for those I work with from time to time. This is always a hit. —AS

Marsha Konken
Sterling, Colorado

Pudding Cake

Makes one 9 by 13-inch cake

1 (15.25-ounce) box cake
  mix (any flavor)
4 eggs
1/2 cup vegetable oil
1 1/4 cups milk
1 (6-ounce) box instant
  pudding mix (any flavor)

Frosting

1 (3-ounce) box instant
  pudding mix (any flavor)
2 cups milk
1 (8-ounce) container frozen
  whipped topping, thawed

Preheat the oven to 350°F. Spray a 9 by 13-inch cake pan with nonstick cooking spray. In a large bowl, mix all of the cake ingredients together with a mixer until smooth. Pour the batter into the prepared pan. Bake for 40 to 45 minutes, until a toothpick inserted into the center of the cake comes out clean. Set the pan on a wire rack to cool completely.

To make the frosting, combine the pudding mix, milk, and whipped topping and beat on medium-low speed until smooth. Frost the cake and chill until ready to serve. ■

This is such an easy cake to put together. Try different combinations of cake and pudding mixes. You can even top the frosting with toffee candy bits or crushed pecans, if desired. —MK

cakes & cheesecakes

Karen Wold-Wallis
Oceanside, California

Karen's Kwik Chocolate
Decadence Cake

Makes one 10-inch Bundt cake

Unsweetened cocoa
powder, for dusting
1 (15.25-ounce) box
chocolate fudge cake mix

1 (12-ounce) package
double-chocolate chips

Generously grease a 10-inch microwavable Bundt pan and dust with unsweetened cocoa powder.

Prepare the cake mix batter according to package directions. Fold in the chocolate chips. Pour the batter into the prepared pan. Bake in the microwave at 50 percent power for 11 minutes. If using a microwave without a turntable, give the pan a half turn. Continue microwaving for 4 to 5 minutes at full power. Let cool for 10 minutes on a flat surface and then turn out onto a serving dish. ■

This unique cake makes its own topping in the microwave and takes only 15 minutes to bake! I came up with this recipe more than thirty years ago when my husband and I were first married and we bought our first microwave oven. I've experimented with other kinds of cake mix and additions other than chocolate chips and it has always come out great! —KWW

Nadia Salmon
Guayaquil, Ecuador

Brownie Cake

Makes one 8-inch round cake

2 1/2 cups sugar
1 cup butter, softened
5 eggs
1 teaspoon vanilla extract
1 cup all-purpose flour
1 teaspoon baking soda

1 cup unsweetened
 cocoa powder
1 cup chopped nuts,
 such as walnuts or
 pecans (optional)

Preheat the oven to 375°F. Grease an 8-inch round cake pan.

In a medium bowl, beat the sugar and butter on medium speed for 5 minutes. Add the eggs one at a time, followed by the vanilla. In a small bowl, whisk together the flour, baking soda, and cocoa. Add them to the batter and mix for 10 minutes. The batter should be spongey. Use a spatula to fold in the nuts. Pour the batter into the prepared pan.

Bake for 30 minutes. After 30 minutes, turn off the oven and leave the cake inside for 30 minutes to cool. ■

You can serve this with tea, coffee, or ice cream. Do not refrigerate it. Although this is called Brownie Cake, the texture is more like a brownie because of the small amount of flour. You can add an extra 1/2 cup of flour to make it more cake-like. If using salted nuts, you may prefer to use semisweet cocoa powder instead of unsweetened. —NS

cakes & cheesecakes

Lorraine Tyler
Richwood, Texas

Edith's

Dark Chocolate Cake

Makes one 9 by 13-inch cake

1 cup butter or margarine

1 cup water

2 cups sugar

2 cups all-purpose flour

1/4 cup dark unsweetened
cocoa powder

1 teaspoon baking soda

1/2 teaspoon ground
cinnamon

1/2 cup buttermilk

2 eggs

1 tablespoon vanilla extract

Icing

1 cup butter or margarine

6 tablespoons dark
unsweetened
cocoa powder

6 tablespoons milk

4 cups confectioners'
sugar, sifted

1 teaspoon vanilla extract

1 cup pecan halves

Preheat the oven to 350°F. Spray a 9 by 13-inch baking pan with nonstick cooking spray.

In a small saucepan over low heat, melt the butter with the water. In a large bowl, whisk together the dry ingredients. Add the butter mixture, buttermilk, eggs, and vanilla and mix well. Pour the batter into the prepared pan and bake for 30 to 35 minutes, until a toothpick inserted into the center comes out clean.

While the cake is baking, make the icing. In a large saucepan over medium-low heat, combine the butter, cocoa powder, and milk and cook, stirring constantly, until it begins to bubble. Remove from the heat and stir in the confectioners' sugar and vanilla until smooth. Pour the icing over the hot cake in the pan. Sprinkle the pecans across the top of the cake. Let set before serving. ∎

In the 1970s, I babysat for a lady named Edith who had four little boys. She made this cake for birthdays and special occasions. I tweaked the recipe a little to suit my family's tastes. It is my mother's favorite cake, and I have made it for her birthday many times. You can use walnuts instead of pecans, and milk chocolate cocoa powder instead of dark chocolate. —LT

cakes & cheesecakes

Stephanie Barken
Chesterfield, Missouri

Cocoa Whipped Cream Cake

Makes one 10-inch cake

1 (16-ounce) box angel
food cake mix
1 cup sugar
5 tablespoons unsweetened
cocoa powder

2 cups heavy
whipping cream
1 teaspoon vanilla extract

Prepare the cake mix according to package instructions. Let cool completely, then slice it into two layers.

While the cake is cooling, prepare the icing. In a large bowl, mix the sugar, cocoa powder, and whipping cream. Refrigerate in the bowl for 1 hour. Beat with a mixer on medium speed until soft peaks form, and then gently fold in the vanilla. Spread some icing across the bottom cake layer. Add the top layer and then frost the entire cake. Keep refrigerated until ready to serve. ■

This is the Schoeneberg family's traditional birthday cake. I think my mother got the recipe from her mother-in-law, and she makes it for everyone's birthday except her own because she doesn't like it. We increase the icing recipe by half to make sure there is a lot. My Aunt Dot would triple it and freeze the extra for a frozen "mousse" later. It is worth searching for Droste cocoa powder. It's always been our favorite, so we always refer to this as Droste's Cake. —SB

Shari Porter
Pickering, Ontario

Chocolate Éclair Cake

Makes one 9 by 13-inch cake

1 (14.4-ounce) box graham
crackers, crushed
2 (3.4-ounce) boxes instant
vanilla pudding mix
3 1/2 cups whole milk
1 (8-ounce) container frozen
whipped topping, thawed

Frosting

1 1/2 cups confectioners'
sugar
1/2 cup unsweetened
cocoa powder
3 tablespoons butter, softened
1/3 cup whole milk
2 teaspoons light corn syrup
2 teaspoons vanilla extract

Butter the bottom of a 9 by 13-inch baking pan. Line the pan with one-third of the crushed graham crackers.

In a medium bowl with a mixer, beat the vanilla pudding and milk at medium speed for 3 minutes. Fold in the whipped topping. Pour half of the pudding mixture over the graham cracker crumbs. Place another layer of graham cracker crumbs on top of the pudding layer. Pour the remaining half of the pudding mixture over the top, then cover with the remaining graham cracker crumbs. Place the pan in the refrigerator to chill.

To make the frosting, whisk together the confectioners' sugar and cocoa powder in a medium bowl. Add the butter and milk and mix well. Add the corn syrup and vanilla and stir until creamy. Frost the top of the cake. Refrigerate for at least 12 hours or up to 1 day before serving. ■

I make this cool, easy dessert every summer. —SP

cakes & cheesecakes

Jan Green
Muskogee, Oklahoma

Mom's
German Chocolate
Cake and Frosting

Makes one 8-inch cake

1 (4-ounce) bar
  German chocolate
2 1/3 cups all-purpose
  flour, sifted
1 1/2 cups sugar
1 teaspoon baking soda
1/2 teaspoon baking powder
1/2 teaspoon salt
2/3 cup butter, softened
3/4 cup plus 1/4 cup
  buttermilk, divided
1 teaspoon vanilla extract
2 eggs

Frosting
4 egg yolks
1 1/4 cups sugar
1 (12-ounce) can
  evaporated milk
1/4 cup butter
Pinch of salt
1 1/2 cups sweetened
  shredded coconut
1 cup chopped pecans

Preheat the oven to 325°F. Line three 8-inch cake pans with parchment paper. Melt the German chocolate in the top of a double boiler over medium heat, then set aside to cool.

In a medium bowl, sift the flour with the sugar, baking soda, baking powder, and salt. In a large bowl with a mixer, beat the butter on medium speed until creamy, and then add the flour mixture, the 3/4 cup of the buttermilk, and the vanilla. Mix gently to moisten the dry ingredients, then beat for 2 minutes on medium speed, occasionally scraping the bowl.

Add the melted chocolate, eggs, and the remaining 1/4 cup of buttermilk. Beat for 1 minute. Pour the batter into the prepared pans. Bake for 35 minutes, or until a toothpick inserted into the center comes out clean. Set the pans on wire racks to cool for 15 minutes. Invert the cakes from the pans and let cool completely on the racks.

While the cakes are cooling, make the frosting. In a large saucepan over medium heat, combine the egg yolks, sugar, evaporated milk, butter, and salt. Stir in the coconut and pecans. Simmer until thick, stirring often. Let cool completely before frosting the cake. Frost between each cake layer, and then frost the sides and top of the stacked cake. ■

Mary Nowlin's German Chocolate Cake was famous in Sallisaw, Oklahoma. She made this for every civic activity, as well as for births, birthdays, and funerals. No one ever beat her out for the highest bid at the Black Diamond Football Cake and Pie Auction. She's been gone for several years now, but the notoriety of her cake lives on! —JG

cakes & cheesecakes

Kimlee Bublitz
Newbury Park, California

Granny Fischer's
Chocolate Angel Torte

Makes 12 servings

4 ounces bittersweet
  chocolate
1 1/2 cups boiling water
2 (0.25-ounce) envelopes
  unflavored gelatin
1/4 cup cold water
6 eggs, separated

2/3 cup sugar
1 teaspoon plus 1/2 teaspoon
  vanilla extract, divided
1 prepared angel food cake,
  cut into 1-inch pieces
1 cup heavy whipping cream
1/4 cup confectioners' sugar

Melt the chocolate in the boiling water. Set aside.

Dissolve the gelatin in the 1/4 cup of cold water, then add it to
the hot chocolate mixture. Let cool until it gels. Beat the egg
yolks in a small bowl, then add to the gelled chocolate mix.

In a large bowl with a mixer, beat the egg whites on medium
speed until stiff. Slowly add the sugar. Beat thoroughly, then
add the 1 teaspoon of the vanilla. Pour the chocolate mixture
into the egg white mixture and fold well; do not beat.

Line the bottom of a round torte pan with the angel food cake
pieces. Pour half of the chocolate mixture on top. Arrange
another layer of cake pieces and pour on the rest of the
chocolate mixture. Refrigerate overnight.

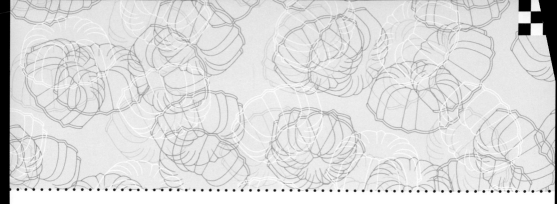

Just before serving the torte, beat the whipping cream on high speed in a large nonmetal bowl and, as it thickens, slowly add the confectioners' sugar and the remaining 1/2 teaspoon of vanilla; continue to beat until, when you raise the beater out, the peak holds its shape.

Gently remove the sides of the torte pan and frost the torte with the whipped cream. Cut the cake into squares—not pie shapes—for optimal pieces. Cut long 2-inch lines across the whole cake, then 1-inch lines in the other direction. Refrigerate any leftovers and eat within 3 days. ■

My granny, Selma Fischer, was born in Germany in the late 1800s and arrived in the United States in 1895. She made this for our holiday celebrations for as long as I can remember. It wasn't a holiday without this torte, and if someone made this for you outside of the holidays, it was a special treat. It wows everyone who tastes it. Don't try to skimp and use artificial whipped toppings. —KB

cakes & cheesecakes

Ann Deakers
San Diego, California

Chocolate Angel Cake
Dessert

Makes one 8-inch cake

1 (12-ounce) package
   chocolate chips
2 teaspoons sugar
3 eggs, separated
2 cups heavy
   whipping cream

1 prepared angel food cake
1 (2.25-ounce) package
   sliced almonds, or colored
   sprinkles, for garnish

Butter an 8-inch springform pan (or an 8 by 12-inch pan).

In the top of a double boiler over medium heat, melt the chocolate chips and sugar, stirring often. In a small bowl, beat the egg yolks. Remove the chocolate mixture from the heat, stir in the yolks, and then let cool for 5 minutes.

In a medium bowl with a mixer, beat the egg whites on medium speed until stiff. In another medium bowl, whip the whipping cream. Fold the egg whites and whipped cream into the chocolate mixture.

Break the angel food cake into bite-size pieces. Place half of the angel food cake in the bottom of the prepared pan. Pour half of the chocolate mixture over the cake. Place the remaining pieces of the angel food cake on top of the chocolate mixture, then top with the remaining chocolate. Garnish with sliced almonds or colored sprinkles. Refrigerate overnight. Cut into small squares or wedges to serve. ■

This is our family birthday cake. —AD

Gloria Fox
Sun City Center, Florida

Truly Different Cupcakes

Makes 24 cupcakes

4 (1-ounce) squares
   semisweet chocolate
1 cup margarine
1/2 teaspoon butter
   flavoring
1 1/2 cups chopped
   pecans or walnuts

1 3/4 cups sugar
1 cup all-purpose flour
4 eggs
1 teaspoon vanilla extract
Confectioners' sugar, for
   dusting (optional)

Preheat the oven to 325°F. Line muffin pans with 24 paper liners.

In a small saucepan over low heat, melt the chocolate and margarine. Stir in the butter flavoring and pecans. Remove from the heat.

In a medium bowl, combine the sugar, flour, eggs, and vanilla and mix well. Carefully fold in the chocolate–nut mixture. Fill each liner two-thirds full. Bake for 35 minutes, or until a toothpick inserted into the center of a cupcake comes out clean.

Set the pans on wire racks to cool completely. Dust each cupcake with confectioners' sugar just before serving, if desired. ■

This recipe is from my children's great-grandmother. I've been using it for forty-five years. Every time I use it, it turns out perfect. I also like it because I don't have to drag out the mixer. The cupcakes are more like a cake brownie. —GF

cakes & cheesecakes

21

Teresa Carns
Redwood City, California

Cupcakes au Macaroon

Makes 12 cupcakes

3/4 cup all-purpose flour
1 cup plus 1/3 cup
  sugar, divided
1/2 teaspoon baking powder
1/2 teaspoon salt
6 egg whites
1/2 teaspoon cream of tartar

1/2 teaspoon vanilla extract
1/2 teaspoon almond extract
1 cup sweetened
  shredded coconut
1/2 cup chocolate
  chips (optional)

Preheat the oven to 300°F. Line a muffin pan with 12 paper liners.

Sift the flour, the 1 cup of the sugar, the baking powder, and salt into a large bowl.

In a separate large bowl, beat the egg whites, cream of tartar, and the remaining 1/3 cup of sugar with a mixer on medium speed for 3 to 5 minutes, until fluffy. Add the vanilla and almond extracts. Fold the dry ingredients into the egg white mixture. Fold in the coconut and chocolate chips. Divide the batter evenly among the liners. Bake for 40 minutes, or until a toothpick inserted into the center of a cupcake comes out clean. ∎

I love coconut, vanilla, and almond flavors. I associate them with the following cultures: Portuguese, Hawaiian, Filipino. I am "Ameurasian"—born in America of Dutch, Portuguese, Asian, Irish, and Goanese descent. I look Portuguese, and most Portuguese love sweets and love to eat! —TC

Susan Butterworth
Harper, Texas

German Apple Cake

Makes one 9 by 13-inch cake

2 eggs
2 cups sugar
1 cup vegetable oil
1 teaspoon vanilla extract
1 teaspoon baking soda
2 teaspoons baking powder
1 teaspoon salt

2 1/2 cups all-purpose flour
1 teaspoon ground
cinnamon
3 cups peeled and
chopped apples
1 cup chopped nuts (such
as pecans or walnuts)

Preheat the oven to 350°F. Spray a 9 by 13-inch cake pan with nonstick cooking spray.

In a large bowl with a mixer, beat the eggs lightly, and then add the sugar, oil, vanilla, baking soda, baking powder, salt, flour, and cinnamon. Mix well on medium speed. Use a spatula to fold in the apples and nuts. Pour the batter into the prepared pan. Bake for 55 to 60 minutes, until a toothpick inserted into the center comes out clean. ∎

My mother made this cake every Christmas, as did her mother when she could afford the ingredients. My mother was the baby of eleven children, and my grandfather died when she was two, so Grandma raised them all with the help of her sister, who married my grandpa's brother. —SB

cakes & cheesecakes

Ann Mueller
Olympia, Washington

Pumpkin Cake Roll

Makes one 15-inch roll

3 eggs
2/3 cup pumpkin puree
(not pie filling)
1 teaspoon freshly
squeezed lemon juice
2/3 cup all-purpose flour
2 teaspoons ground
cinnamon
1 teaspoon baking powder
1 cup sugar
1/2 teaspoon ground
nutmeg

1 teaspoon ground ginger
1/2 teaspoon salt
1 cup finely chopped walnuts
2/3 cup confectioners' sugar

Filling

2 (3-ounce) packages
cream cheese, softened
1/4 cup butter
1 teaspoon vanilla extract
1 cup confectioners' sugar

Preheat the oven to 375°F. Grease and flour a 10 by 15 by 1-inch jelly roll pan.

In a large bowl with a mixer, beat the eggs on high speed for 5 minutes. Add the pumpkin and lemon juice and beat on medium speed until combined.

In a medium bowl, mix together the flour, cinnamon, baking powder, sugar, nutmeg, ginger, and salt. Fold into the pumpkin mixture and blend well. Pour the batter into the prepared jelly roll pan and sprinkle the walnuts on top. Bake for 15 minutes, or until a toothpick inserted into the center comes out clean.

Coat a clean, lint-free dish towel with the confectioners' sugar, place the cake on it, and roll up the cake with the towel still around it. Let cool completely.

While the cake is cooling, make the filling. In a medium bowl, beat the cream cheese, butter, vanilla, and confectioners' sugar until smooth. Unroll the cooled cake and set aside the dish towel. Spread the filling on top of the cake and roll it back up without the towel. Place the roll seam side down on a baking sheet and refrigerate until ready to serve. To serve, cut the roll into 1-inch slices. ■

This recipe is from our daughter-in-law. She makes it for Thanksgiving or Christmas. I've taken it to several get-togethers, and it's always a hit. If you use a 15-ounce can of pumpkin, you can make two rolls. —AM

cakes & cheesecakes

Lisa Simmons
Cape Girardeau, Missouri

Cinnamon Supper Cake

Makes one 9 by 13-inch cake

1 1/2 cups sugar
1/2 cup vegetable oil
2 eggs
1 cup 2 percent milk
2 cups all-purpose flour
1 tablespoon baking powder
2 teaspoons vanilla extract
1/4 teaspoon salt

Topping

1/2 cup margarine, melted
1 (16-ounce) package
   confectioners' sugar
1/4 cup ground cinnamon

Preheat the oven to 375°F. Spray a 9 by 13-inch cake pan with nonstick cooking spray.

In a large bowl with a mixer, beat the sugar, oil, and eggs on medium speed. Add the milk and the rest of the cake ingredients. Beat for 2 to 3 minutes, until smooth. Pour the batter into the prepared pan. Bake for 20 to 30 minutes, until the top is golden brown.

To make the topping, pour the melted margarine over the hot cake. In a medium bowl, mix the confectioners' sugar and cinnamon together and sprinkle over the cake. The topping will be fluffy and thick. Let cool slightly before serving ∎

When I was dating my soon-to-be husband, his mom used to bake this delicious cake for all the "kids." That was almost thirty years ago. Now my husband bakes this every year on Christmas morning for me and our kids, who are adults now. —LS

Tam Veilleux
Freeport, Maine

Claire's
Blueberry Cake

Makes one 8-inch cake

1 cup plus 1/4 cup
   sugar, divided
2 eggs, separated
1/2 cup lard
1/4 teaspoon salt
1 teaspoon vanilla extract

1 1/2 cups plus 1 teaspoon
   all-purpose flour, divided
1 teaspoon baking powder
1/3 cup milk
1 cup fresh or thawed
   frozen blueberries

Preheat the oven to 350°F. Spray an 8-inch square baking dish.

In a large bowl, mix together the 1 cup of the sugar, the egg yolks, lard, salt, vanilla, the 1 1/2 cups of the flour, the baking powder, and milk. Be careful not to overmix. Fold the egg whites into the batter. In a small bowl, toss the blueberries with the remaining 1 teaspoon of flour. Gently fold the blueberries into the batter. Pour the batter into the prepared dish and sprinkle the top of the batter with the remaining 1/4 cup of sugar. Bake for 35 to 40 minutes, until the top is golden brown and a toothpick inserted into the center comes out clean. ■

This is a staple for me and my sisters-in-law. One time my mother-in-law left her husband at home for a week and asked if we would mind helping him with dinners. That Thursday I served him a baked chicken dinner and this cake. I asked him how he liked it, and he replied that he surely had better like it since the other ladies had served the exact same thing! —TV

cakes & cheesecakes

27

Cheryl Henry
Steele, Missouri

Strawberry Cake

Makes one 9 by 13-inch cake

1 (18.25-ounce) box
white cake mix
1/2 cup water
1 (3-ounce) box strawberry-
flavored gelatin
1/2 cup strawberry
juice, drained from
frozen sweetened
sliced strawberries
3 eggs
1 cup vegetable oil

Icing

1 (16-ounce) package
confectioners' sugar
1/2 cup butter or
margarine, softened
1/2 cup mashed strawberries,
from frozen sweetened
sliced strawberries

Preheat the oven to 350°F. Grease and flour a 9 by 13-inch
cake pan.

In a large bowl, combine the cake mix, water, gelatin, strawberry
juice, eggs, and oil. Beat for 2 minutes with a mixer on medium
speed. Pour the batter into the prepared pan. Bake for 33 to 38
minutes, until a toothpick inserted into the middle comes out
clean. Set the pan on a wire rack to cool.

While the cake is baking, make the icing. In a medium bowl, mix together the confectioners' sugar, butter, and mashed strawberries, and beat on medium speed until well combined. Ice the cake in the pan while it is still warm. Refrigerate any leftovers. ■

I make this cake for my daughter every year for her birthday. It is her favorite! She loves it served with her birthday dinner, but she also loves it the next day, served cold from the refrigerator for breakfast with an ice-cold glass of milk! My son-in-law has even learned to make this cake for her. He tops it with fresh chocolate-covered strawberries. —CH

cakes & cheesecakes

Jacqueline Roddy
Inverness, Florida

Cherry Upside-Down Cake

Makes one 9 by 13-inch cake

3 tablespoons butter
2 cups sugar
2 eggs
2 (14.5-ounce) cans
  tart pitted cherries in
  syrup, with the syrup
  from 1 can reserved

2 teaspoons baking soda
2 cups all-purpose flour
Whipped cream, for garnish

Preheat the oven to 350°F. Spray a 9 by 13-inch baking pan.

In a large bowl with a mixer, cream the butter, sugar, and eggs on medium speed. Add the reserved syrup from 1 can of cherries. Add the baking soda and flour and mix well.

Pour the drained cherries across the bottom of the prepared pan. Pour the cake batter on top. Place in the oven immediately so the cherries do not rise to the top. Bake for 40 to 50 minutes, until a toothpick inserted into the center comes out clean. Serve warm with whipped cream, if desired. ■

My mom brought this recipe with us when we moved from a farm in Missouri to Miami, Florida. She made it for me the day I brought my new son home from the hospital. My son's family now has the recipe, so it will keep moving up the family tree for years to come. —JR

Nancy Graeb
Wray, Colorado

Peachy Pecan Cake

Makes one 9 by 13-inch cake

1 (29-ounce) can sliced
  peaches in syrup
1 (15.25-ounce) box
  butter pecan cake mix

1/2 cup butter or
  margarine, melted
1/2 cup sweetened
  shredded coconut
1/2 cup chopped pecans

Preheat the oven to 350°F. Grease a 9 by 13-inch baking pan.

Pour the peaches and their syrup into the bottom of the pan. Pour the cake mix on top. Drizzle the butter over that, then sprinkle the coconut and pecans across the top. Bake for 50 to 60 minutes, until a toothpick inserted into the center comes out clean. Let cool on a wire rack. ■

This is a quick dessert that tastes great! —NG

cakes & cheesecakes

Ellen Miller
Beatrice, Nebraska

Orange Slice Cake

Makes one 10-inch cake

1 cup butter

2 cups sugar

5 eggs

1/2 teaspoon baking soda

3/4 cup buttermilk

3 1/2 cups plus 1/2 cup all-
purpose flour, divided

1 teaspoon salt

1 teaspoon vanilla extract

1 pound orange slice candies,
cut into small pieces

1 (16-ounce) package
chopped dates

2 cups pecans, chopped

1 cup sweetened
shredded coconut

Glaze

2 cups confectioners'
sugar, sifted

1 cup orange juice

Preheat the oven to 250°F. Grease and flour a 10-inch tube pan.

In a large bowl, cream the butter and sugar together until fluffy.
Add the eggs one at a time, mixing well after each addition.
In a small bowl, dissolve the baking soda in the buttermilk. In
a separate large bowl, whisk together the 3 1/2 cups of the
flour and the salt. Add the flour mixture to the butter mixture,
alternating with the buttermilk mixture, beginning and ending
with flour. Stir in the vanilla.

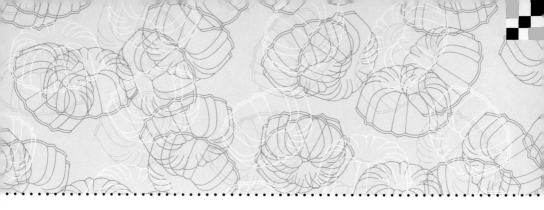

In a medium bowl, toss the orange slices, dates, and pecans with the remaining 1/2 cup of flour until coated. Stir in the coconut until well combined. Add the mixture to the batter and stir until well combined. Pour the batter into the prepared tube pan and bake for 2 1/2 to 3 hours, until a toothpick inserted into the center comes out clean.

During the last few minutes of baking, prepare the glaze. In a medium bowl, combine the confectioners' sugar and orange juice and whisk until smooth. Pour the glaze over the hot cake. Leave the cake in the pan overnight. Invert onto a serving plate to serve. ∎

This was my mammaw's recipe. I used to love going through her recipes when I visited her. I was given her recipes when she passed away, and I found this written on an old piece of notebook paper. —EM

cakes & cheesecakes

Susan Rogers
Manhattan, Kansas

Persimmon Pudding Cake

Makes one 8-inch cake

1 cup persimmon pulp (from
about 3 large persimmons)

2 eggs, beaten

1 cup milk, plus
more if needed

1 1/2 tablespoons
butter, melted

1 cup all-purpose flour

1/2 teaspoon baking soda

1/4 teaspoon ground
cinnamon

1/4 teaspoon ground nutmeg

3/4 cup sugar

1/2 teaspoon salt

1/2 cup raisins or chopped
nuts (such as pecans or
walnuts; optional)

Whipped topping or
vanilla ice cream, for
serving (optional)

Preheat the oven to 350°F. Butter an 8-inch square baking pan.

In a large bowl, mix the persimmon pulp and eggs. Add the milk and butter. In a separate bowl, sift and mix the flour, baking soda, cinnamon, nutmeg, sugar, and salt. Add the dry ingredients to the persimmon mixture and blend until a soft batter forms; add more milk if the batter is stiff. Fold in the raisins. Pour the batter into the prepared pan. Bake for 30 to 45 minutes, until a toothpick inserted in the center comes out clean. Let cool on a wire rack. Serve with whipped topping, vanilla ice cream, or by itself. ■

I was little the first time I bit into an unripe persimmon. My mom told me that with patience, even a bitter, unripe fruit could turn into a sweet, rich, and yummy dessert. I never forgot that life lesson. —SR

Susan Ego
Corte Madera, California

Orange Cream Cake

Makes one 9 by 13-inch cake

1 (15.25-ounce) box
white cake mix with
pudding in the mix
1 (3-ounce) box orange-
flavored gelatin
1 cup boiling water
1/2 cup cold water

Frosting

1 (3.4-ounce) box instant
vanilla pudding mix
1 cup milk
1 (8-ounce) container frozen
whipped topping, thawed
1 teaspoon vanilla extract
1 teaspoon orange extract

Spray a 9 by 13-inch cake pan with nonstick cooking spray. Prepare and bake the cake mix according to package directions. Set the pan on a wire rack to cool completely.

In a small saucepan, dissolve the orange gelatin in the boiling water, stirring well. Add the cold water. Use a wooden spoon handle to poke holes in the cake, then pour the gelatin mixture over the cake.

To make the frosting, beat the pudding mix and milk in a medium bowl with a mixer on medium-low speed until thickened. Mix in the whipped topping and vanilla and orange extracts. Frost the cake and refrigerate. Serve cold. ■

This is a great summertime dessert, as it is served cold. It tastes just like the orange Creamsicle bars we had as kids from the ice-cream trucks. —SE

cakes & cheesecakes

Anna Marie Penix
Tulsa, Oklahoma

Mimi's Three-Layer
Carrot Cake

Makes one 8-inch cake

3 cups shredded carrots
2 cups all-purpose
   flour, sifted
1 1/4 cups vegetable oil
2 teaspoons ground
   cinnamon
2 teaspoons baking soda
1 teaspoon salt
4 eggs
2 cups sugar

Icing

1 (8-ounce) package
   cream cheese, softened
1 (16-ounce) package
   confectioners' sugar
1/2 cup margarine
1 teaspoon vanilla extract

Preheat the oven to 325°F. Cut waxed paper circles to fit into the bottoms of three 8-inch round metal cake pans. Grease and flour the sides of the pans.

In a large bowl, blend all of the cake batter ingredients until smooth. Divide the batter evenly among the three prepared cake pans. Bake for 40 minutes, or until a toothpick inserted into the center comes out clean. Set on wire racks to cool completely, then invert the cakes to remove them from the pans and carefully peel off the waxed paper circles.

While the cakes are cooling, prepare the icing. In a large bowl, mix the cream cheese, confectioners' sugar, margarine, and vanilla until smooth. Frost the first cake layer, then top it with another layer and frost that, then top with the third layer and frost the sides and top of the cake. Keep the cake refrigerated until serving, but set it on the counter for 5 to 10 minutes before slicing. ■

This is a much-requested favorite among my entire family. My mom ("Mimi") got the recipe years ago from a friend. I always ask for it on my birthday! Many other carrot cake recipes include raisins, pineapple, or coconut, but the simplicity and deliciousness of this pure carrot cake keeps everyone coming back for more! You can add chopped pecans to the cake batter or press them into the sides of the cake after frosting. —AMP

cakes & cheesecakes

Mary Engelbreit
St. Louis, Missouri

Margie's
Cheesecake

Makes one 9-inch cake

Crust

1 cup graham
cracker crumbs
1/4 cup sugar
1/2 teaspoon ground
cinnamon
1/4 cup butter or
margarine, melted

Filling

2 (8-ounce) packages
cream cheese, softened
1/2 cup sugar
3 eggs

Topping

2 cups sour cream
1/4 cup sugar
1 teaspoon vanilla extract

Whipped cream, for garnish

Preheat the oven to 375°F. Spray a 9-inch springform pan with nonstick cooking spray. In a small bowl, combine the crust ingredients and mix well. Spread in the bottom of the springform pan.

In a medium bowl, combine the filling ingredients and beat until smooth. Spread the mixture on top of the crust. Bake for 20 minutes, then remove from oven and let cool for 1 hour.

For the topping, preheat the oven to 475°F. In a medium bowl, combine the sour cream, sugar, and vanilla and mix well. Top the cake with the mixture. Bake for 10 minutes. Let the cheesecake cool completely for 1 hour. When cool, cover in plastic wrap and chill for 2 to 3 hours before serving.

Serve cold and garnish with whipped cream. ■

When I was a little girl, my mother got this recipe
from her neighbor Margie. She was an amazing baker,
and this cheesecake became a neighborhood favorite.
Other recipes I have tried over the years just don't seem
to come close. It's still the only one I ever make. —ME

Alysmay Quinton
Reno, Nevada

Easy Cheesecake

Makes one 9 by 13-inch cheesecake

Crust

1/2 cup margarine, melted
1/4 cup packed brown sugar
1/4 cup chopped nuts (such
as pecans or walnuts)
1 cup all-purpose flour

Filling

2 envelopes whipped topping
mix, such as Dream Whip
1 cup milk
1 (8-ounce) package
cream cheese, softened
1 cup confectioners' sugar

Topping

1 (3-ounce) box raspberry-
or cherry-flavored gelatin
1 (3-ounce) box cook-
and-serve (not instant)
vanilla pudding mix
2 1/2 cups water
2 cups fresh or frozen
raspberries or strawberries

Preheat the oven to 350°F.

In a medium bowl, combine all of the ingredients for the crust. Press the crust into the bottom and a little up the sides of a 9 by 13-inch baking pan. Bake for 10 minutes. Set on a wire rack to cool completely.

To make the filling, beat together the whipped topping mix and milk in a medium bowl until thick. Add the cream cheese and confectioners' sugar and blend well. Pour the filling onto the cooled crust.

To make the topping, dissolve the gelatin and pudding in the water in a medium saucepan and cook to a rolling boil, stirring constantly. Remove from the heat and stir in the fruit. Let cool slightly, then pour over the cheesecake. Refrigerate for at least 2 hours before serving. ■

This recipe was given to me more than thirty years ago for a church dinner by my mother-in-law, Dorothy Quinton, who liked to make up her own recipes. It was so easy that I have always made it for Thanksgiving and Christmas dinners, and it is always a favorite. —AQ

Betsy Hada
El Sobrante, California

Three-Layer
Lemon Cheesecake
with Raspberry Sauce

Makes one 10-inch cheesecake

Crust

2 1/2 cups crushed
  cinnamon graham crackers
6 tablespoons butter, melted

Filling

3 (8-ounce) packages
  cream cheese, softened
1 1/3 cups sugar
3 eggs, beaten
1/4 cup freshly squeezed
  lemon juice
1 tablespoon grated
  lemon zest
2 teaspoons vanilla extract

Topping

2 cups sour cream
2 tablespoons sugar
1 teaspoon vanilla extract

Glaze

3/4 cup water
1/3 cup freshly squeezed
  lemon juice
2 egg yolks
1/2 cup sugar
2 tablespoons cornstarch
1/4 teaspoon salt
1 tablespoon butter
2 teaspoons grated
  lemon zest

Raspberry Sauce

1 (16-ounce) bag frozen
  raspberries, thawed
2 tablespoons raspberry
  liqueur or raspberry
  brandy (optional)

Preheat the oven to 350°F. To make the crust, combine the graham cracker crumbs and butter in a medium bowl and mix well. Press into the bottom of a 10-inch springform pan. Bake for 5 minutes. Set on a wire rack to cool for 5 minutes. Leave the oven on.

To make the filling, place the cream cheese in a large bowl and beat with a mixer on medium speed until fluffy. Add the sugar

and beat for 2 to 3 minutes. Beat in the eggs one at a time. Mix in the lemon juice, zest, and vanilla. Pour the filling into the baked crust. Bake for 45 to 60 minutes, until only the center (about 3 inches in) remains unset. Transfer to a rack to cool slightly and gently press down the edges of the cheesecake a bit so that if the cake sinks, it won't have a hole in the center. Leave the oven on.

To make the topping, blend the sour cream, sugar, and vanilla in a medium bowl until combined. Spread the mixture on top of the slightly cooled filling. Bake at 350°F for 15 minutes. Set on a rack to cool for 30 minutes, then chill in the refrigerator. Run a warm knife around the edges of the pan to loosen the cheesecake before unmolding.

To make the glaze, combine the water, lemon juice, egg yolks, sugar, cornstarch, and salt in a small saucepan over medium heat. Cook, stirring constantly, until the mixture starts to boil, about 10 minutes. Remove from the heat and stir in the butter and zest. Let cool completely, then spread the glaze on top of the cheesecake.

To make the raspberry sauce, puree the thawed raspberries in a blender. Add the raspberry liqueur and pulse to mix. To serve, pour a small puddle of raspberry sauce in the center of a dessert plate. Place a slice of the cheesecake on top of the sauce. ■

Once, when my husband and I were both out of work, I baked cheesecakes as gifts instead of buying gifts. Now, no one will allow me to give them anything else! —BH

cakes & cheesecakes

Kay Walker
Marietta, Georgia

White Chocolate–Raspberry Cheesecake

Makes one 9-inch cheesecake

Crust
1 1/2 cups crushed
　graham crackers
1/4 cup sugar
1/2 cup butter, melted

Filling
4 (8-ounce) packages
　cream cheese, softened
3/4 cup sugar
4 large eggs
1 1/2 tablespoons
　vanilla extract

1/4 cup sour cream
1/2 cup plus 1/2
　cup raspberry
　preserves (preferably
　seedless), divided
4 ounces white
　chocolate, melted

Topping (optional)
2 (3.5-ounce) bars
　white chocolate
Canned whipped cream

Preheat the oven to 325°F and place a rack in the center.

To make the crust, mix the crushed graham crackers, sugar, and melted butter in a medium bowl. Press into the bottom and sides of a 9-inch springform pan. Bake for 8 minutes, then let cool completely. Leave the oven on.

To make the filling, beat the cream cheese and sugar in a large bowl until well blended. Add the eggs one at a time, mixing after each addition. Add the vanilla, sour cream, and 1/2 cup of the raspberry preserves. Stir until well blended, but do not overmix. Add the melted white chocolate and blend well. Pour the remaining 1/2 cup of preserves on top and briefly stir in circles

with a spoon to marble it. Drag a knife through it to marble it a little more. Do not fully mix in the preserves. Pour the cheesecake batter into the prepared cooled crust.

Bake for 1 hour 15 minutes. Turn off the oven, partially open the oven door, and let the cheesecake rest for 15 minutes. Transfer the cheesecake to a wire rack. Immediately run a knife around the edges of the cheesecake but leave it in the pan. Let cool completely. Cover with plastic and refrigerate for at least 8 hours.

If you want to jazz up the cheesecake and cover any little cracks or splits in the top, use a potato peeler to shave curls from the bars of white chocolate. Spread the curls over the center of the cheesecake. Pipe a decorative border of whipped cream around the edges. Serve immediately. ■

This is easy, but it looks and tastes like something a five-star restaurant would make. It is always the first dessert to disappear during family functions, and everyone in my family requests it every Christmas. —XW

cakes & cheesecakes

Charlene Wooden
Easthampton, Massachusetts

Cranberry-Apple-Carrot Cake

Makes one 10-inch Bundt cake

1 1/3 cups sugar

2 eggs

1/2 cup vegetable oil

2 1/2 cups all-purpose flour

1 tablespoon baking powder

2 teaspoons baking soda

1/2 teaspoon ground
cinnamon

2 teaspoons ground
coriander

2 cups diced apples

1 cup shredded carrots

1 cup chopped fresh
cranberries

1/2 cup raisins

1 cup chopped walnuts

Preheat the oven to 375°F. Spray a Bundt pan with nonstick cooking spray.

In a large bowl, cream the sugar, eggs, and oil. In a medium bowl, combine the flour, baking powder, baking soda, cinnamon, and coriander and mix thoroughly. Add the dry ingredients to the sugar mixture and beat until smooth. Gently fold in the apples, carrots, cranberries, raisins, and nuts. Pour the batter into the prepared pan. Bake for 1 hour or until a toothpick inserted into the center comes out clean. ■

I have had this recipe since my children were very young. I always felt that if I gave them a slice of this when they were running out the door to the school bus, having refused to eat breakfast, I was giving them somewhat of a good start while allowing them to think I was feeding them dessert for breakfast. —CW

Bethane Smith
Saint Johns, Michigan

Mint Swirl Cheesecake

Makes one 9-inch cheesecake

1 1/2 cups crushed
crème-filled chocolate
sandwich cookies

2 tablespoons butter, melted

3 (8-ounce) packages
cream cheese, softened

3/4 cup sugar

1/4 cup all-purpose flour

1 teaspoon vanilla extract

1/2 cup sour cream

1/2 cup heavy
whipping cream

3 eggs, beaten

1 to 3 drops peppermint
extract, to taste

Food coloring of
choice (optional)

Hot fudge sauce or
chocolate curls, for garnish

Preheat the oven to 350°F. Mix the crushed cookies and butter in the bottom of a 9-inch springform pan. Press down on the sides and bottom to form a crust. Bake for 5 minutes. Leave the oven on.

In a large bowl with a mixer, beat the cream cheese, sugar, flour, and vanilla until creamy. Add the sour cream and whipping cream and continue to mix. Slowly add the eggs and mix thoroughly. Pour three-quarters of the batter into the crust. Add the peppermint extract and food color to the remaining batter and mix well. Drizzle onto the cheesecake batter in the pan. Use a knife to pull from edge to edge, swirling the mint batter into the vanilla batter. Bake for 55 minutes; the center should not be quite set. Let cool on a wire rack. Garnish with the hot fudge sauce or chocolate curls. Refrigerate any leftovers. ∎

This recipe won third place in a cooking contest. —BS

cakes & cheesecakes

Good apple pies are a
considerable part of our
domestic happiness.

—Jane Austen

Pies, Tarts, Cobblers & Crisps

Amy Gethins
Richmond, Virginia

Italian Prune Plum Pie

Makes one 9-inch pie

5 to 6 cups pitted, sliced
  Italian prune plums
1 1/4 cups sugar
1/2 teaspoon salt
3 tablespoons quick-
  cooking tapioca
3/4 teaspoon ground allspice
2 tablespoons butter, sliced

Crust

1 cup all-purpose flour
1/4 teaspoon salt
1/2 cup cold butter, cut
  into 1/2-inch pieces
3 to 4 tablespoons ice water

Vanilla ice cream, for serving

Preheat the oven to 450°F. Spray an 8-inch square baking dish with nonstick cooking spray.

Place the plums in the prepared dish. In a small bowl, combine the sugar, salt, tapioca, and allspice. Sprinkle the mixture over the plums. Gently shake the dish to distribute the mixture. Dot the top with the butter.

To make the crust, whisk the flour and salt in a large bowl. Use a pastry cutter or fork to cut in the butter until the mixture forms coarse crumbs. Gently stir in the water, 1 tablespoon at a time, until the mixture begins to clump together. Use your hands to press and shape the mixture into a flat disk. Place the disk on a lightly floured surface and roll into a 12-inch circle.

Cover the baking dish with the crust. Trim the crust 2 inches larger than the dish and turn the crust under and flute the edges. Bake for 30 to 40 minutes, until bubbly and browned. Serve warm with vanilla ice cream. ■

This is just one of the delicious recipes that I learned from my mother-in-law and kindred spirit, Delma. I was blessed to have her in my life, gardening, cooking, and having wonderful chats, and I miss her very much.

Italian prune plum season is from the end of August into September. My birthday is September 3, and I choose this pie over cake every time. —AG

pies, tarts, cobblers & crisps

Kathleen Brown
Victoria, British Columbia, Canada

Apple Sheet Pie

Makes 32 servings

Crust

3 cups all-purpose flour

3/4 teaspoon salt

1 1/2 cups butter-flavored shortening

1 egg

1 egg yolk

1 1/2 tablespoons freshly squeezed lemon juice

7 1/2 tablespoons cold water

Filling

1 1/2 cups sugar

3/4 teaspoon salt

5 tablespoons all-purpose flour

3 tablespoons instant tapioca

1 tablespoon ground cinnamon

3/4 teaspoon ground nutmeg

8 cups 1/8- to 1/4-inch-thick sliced apples (10 to 12 medium apples)

Frosting

2 tablespoons butter, softened

1 1/2 cups confectioners' sugar

2 teaspoons vanilla extract

Milk, to thin

Preheat the oven to 375°F.

To make the crust, mix the flour, salt, and shortening in a large bowl. In a separate bowl, beat the egg, egg yolk, lemon juice, and water. Add to the flour mixture and form into a dough. Shape into a ball and refrigerate while making the filling.

To make the filling, mix the sugar, salt, flour, tapioca, cinnamon, and nutmeg in a large bowl. Add the apples and toss to coat. Roll out half of the dough onto a 10 by 15-inch jelly roll pan.

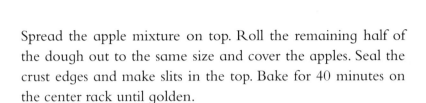

Spread the apple mixture on top. Roll the remaining half of the dough out to the same size and cover the apples. Seal the crust edges and make slits in the top. Bake for 40 minutes on the center rack until golden.

While the pie is baking, make the frosting. In a medium bowl, beat all of the ingredients together until smooth. Frost the pie while still warm. ■

As the chief chef for our church functions growing up, my mother, Ann Armstrong, used our family as guinea pigs for her newfound recipes. Apple sheet pie became both a family and a church kitchen favorite. Now that I am married to a pastor myself, you can be sure this recipe has found its way into many a church dinner/potluck, and it is still one of our family's most-requested desserts. —KB

Joan Brooks
Pensacola, Florida

"Lick Your Plate Clean!"
Chocolate Pie

Makes one 8-inch pie

Crust

1/2 cup plus 2 tablespoons
 crushed graham crackers
1 1/2 tablespoons sugar
3 tablespoons butter, melted

Filling

1 (8-ounce) chocolate
 bar with almonds,
 broken into pieces
1 teaspoon instant
 coffee granules

2 tablespoons hot water
2 to 4 tablespoons strong
 brewed coffee or coffee
 liqueur (optional)
1 (12-ounce) container
 thawed frozen
 whipped topping, plus
 more for garnish

Chocolate shavings, for
 garnish (optional)

Preheat the oven to 350°F. For the crust, mix together the graham crackers, sugar, and butter in a medium bowl. Press the mixture into the bottom and sides of an 8-inch springform pan. Bake for 8 minutes. Let cool completely.

In the top of a double boiler over low heat, combine the chocolate pieces, coffee granules, and hot water. Stir until melted. If it seems too thick, you can add 2 to 4 tablespoons of strong brewed coffee or coffee liqueur. Let cool completely, then fold in the whipped topping.

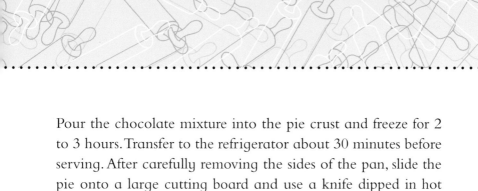

Pour the chocolate mixture into the pie crust and freeze for 2 to 3 hours. Transfer to the refrigerator about 30 minutes before serving. After carefully removing the sides of the pan, slide the pie onto a large cutting board and use a knife dipped in hot water and wiped dry to slice. Garnish with whipped topping and chocolate shavings. ■

This recipe was given to me by a lovely young Navy wife who worked with me at the public library. She also played the oboe! An 8-inch pan makes a nice, deep pie. I have used real whipped cream in place of whipped topping, but it doesn't make a noticeable taste difference except as the garnish. —JB

pies, tarts, cobblers & crisps

Jennifer Creecy
Henderson, Tennessee

Chocolate Meringue Pie

Makes one 9-inch pie

Filling

1 1/2 cups sugar

1/2 cup unsweetened cocoa powder

1/4 teaspoon salt

1/2 cup all-purpose flour

4 egg yolks

1 cup heavy whipping cream

1 cup whole milk

1 teaspoon vanilla extract

1/4 cup salted butter, cut into small chunks

1 (9-inch) prebaked pie crust (regular or deep dish), completely cooled

Meringue

1 (7-ounce) jar marshmallow crème

4 egg whites

1/8 teaspoon salt

1/4 teaspoon cream of tartar

1/2 cup sugar

Preheat the oven to 350°F. To make the filling, combine the sugar, cocoa powder, salt, flour, egg yolks, cream, and milk in a large saucepan over medium heat. Whisk constantly and bring the mixture to a boil. Still whisking, boil until the mixture becomes thick and custard-like. Once the mixture thickens, remove it from the heat and slowly whisk in the vanilla and butter chunks until blended. Pour the custard mixture into the prebaked pie crust.

To make the meringue, place the marshmallow crème in a large bowl. In a separate bowl using a mixer, beat the egg whites, salt, and cream of tartar on medium speed until frothy. Add the sugar, 1 tablespoon at a time, and beat until glossy, stiff peaks form. Fold 1/2 cup of the egg white mixture into the marshmallow crème. Mix until thoroughly combined. Add in half of the remaining

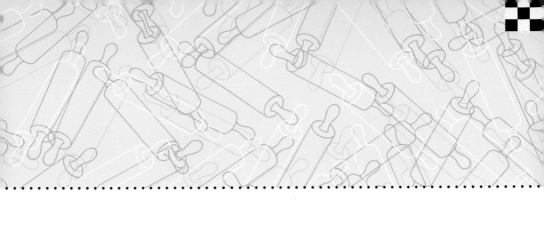

egg white mixture, fold just until combined, and then add in the rest of the egg white mixture, mixing just until combined. Spread the meringue over the filling, sealing the edges against the crust. Bake for 10 to 15 minutes, until the meringue is toasted and golden brown. ∎

The amount of filling will work well with either a regular or a deep-dish pie, as will the meringue. The pie will simply have taller meringue in a regular 9-inch pie plate. The marshmallow crème provides a foolproof, fluffy meringue! —JC

pies, tarts, cobblers & crisps

Mary Kay Abblett
Schererville, Indiana

Raisin Pie

Makes one 9-inch pie

2 cups dark raisins
1/2 cup water or brandy
2 (9-inch) unbaked pie crusts
Butter, for spreading
  and dotting

1 egg
2 tablespoons milk
Raw sugar, for garnish

Preheat the oven to 425°F. In a saucepan over medium-low heat, cook the raisins and water until the liquid evaporates and the mixture is almost gelled. Let cool.

Roll out one of the pie crusts on a lightly floured surface until it is about 12 inches in diameter. Carefully transfer the crust to a 9-inch pie pan and press it in. Prick the bottom of the shell with a fork, then spread butter across the bottom. Pour the raisin mixture into the shell and dot with cubes of butter.

Roll out the second pie crust as you did the first. To create latticework for the top of the pie, cut the pie crust into 1-inch strips. Arrange half the strips in one direction over the pie. Carefully weave the other half of the strips in the other direction, over and under the first set of strips. In a small bowl, whisk the egg and milk until frothy. Slather the egg wash over the pie crust and sprinkle with raw sugar. Bake for 1 hour, or until the center bubbles and the crust turns golden. ■

This recipe came from my mom, Berneicium Clodi-Abblett. "It's the best pie ever, and full of iron," she would say! —MA

Lisa Robason
Corpus Christi, Texas

Spiced Buttermilk Pie

Makes one 9-inch pie

1/2 cup butter
1 1/2 cups sugar
3 eggs
3 tablespoons all-
purpose flour
1 cup buttermilk

1/8 teaspoon ground
nutmeg, preferably
freshly grated
1/2 teaspoon vanilla extract
1/4 teaspoon lemon extract
1 (9-inch) unbaked pie shell

Preheat the oven to 350°F.

In a large bowl, cream the butter and sugar. Add the eggs and flour. Mix well, and stir in the buttermilk, nutmeg, and vanilla and lemon extracts. Pour the mixture onto the pie shell. Bake for 45 minutes, or until set but just a little jiggly in the middle. Let cool completely before slicing and serving. (The center will firm more as it cools.) Refrigerate leftovers. ■

Our family's holiday celebrations wouldn't be
the same without this pie. The nutmeg offers
a subtle flavor that can't be beat! —LR

pies, tarts, cobblers & crisps

Chris Morse
Columbia, South Carolina

Derby Pie

Makes one 10-inch pie

1 (10-inch) unbaked
   pie crust
3/4 cup semisweet
   chocolate chips
2 eggs

1 teaspoon vanilla extract
1/2 cup butter, melted
1 cup sugar
1/2 cup pecan pieces
1/2 cup self-rising flour

Preheat the oven to 350°F. Place the pie crust in a deep-dish pie pan and crimp the edges. Lightly pierce holes in the bottom of the crust with a fork. Sprinkle the chocolate chips into the crust.

In a medium bowl, combine the eggs, vanilla, butter, sugar, pecan pieces, and flour and mix well. Pour the mixture over the chocolate chips. Bake for 45 minutes, or until the center is firm. Let cool completely before slicing and serving. Refrigerate leftovers. ■

This recipe is great warm or cold. I prefer it warm, topped with a scoop of vanilla ice cream. We like to make these for Christmas gifts—they always go over well! —CM

Marsha Konken
Sterling, Colorado

Caramel-Pecan Pie

Makes one 9-inch pie

28 vanilla caramels,
   unwrapped
1/2 cup water
1/4 cup butter
2 eggs, lightly beaten

3/4 cup sugar
1/4 teaspoon salt
1/2 teaspoon vanilla extract
1 cup pecan halves
1 (9-inch) unbaked pie shell

Preheat the oven to 400°F. In a small saucepan, combine the caramels, water, and butter and cook over low heat until the caramels are melted. In a medium bowl, stir together the eggs, sugar, salt, and vanilla. Slowly add the egg mixture to the caramel sauce, stirring until well blended. Stir in the pecans. Pour the mixture into the pie shell.

Bake for 10 minutes, then decrease the oven temperature to 350°F and bake for another 20 minutes. Let cool completely before slicing and serving. ∎

I got this recipe from my aunt and have made it several times. It's always a hit with family and friends. It can be topped with whipped topping or ice cream, if desired. —MK

pies, tarts, cobblers & crisps

61

Sue Manyak
Long Beach, California

Pecan Tarts

Makes 24 tarts

Shells

1/2 cup butter, softened
1 (3-ounce) package
  cream cheese
1 cup all-purpose flour

Filling

1 egg
3/4 cup packed brown sugar
3/4 cup chopped pecans
1 tablespoon butter, melted
1 teaspoon vanilla extract

Preheat the oven to 375°F. Spray mini muffin pans with nonstick cooking spray. Lightly flour the pan if necessary to keep the shells from sticking.

To make the shells, cream the butter and cream cheese in a medium bowl, then add the flour and mix until a batter forms. Divide the batter into 24 equal-size balls. Carefully press and flatten one ball into each cup of the prepared pan. Set aside.

To make the filling, blend all of the ingredients together until smooth. Divide the mixture equally among the 24 shells. Bake for 15 to 20 minutes, until the tarts are lightly browned. Let cool slightly in the pan and then transfer the tarts to a wire rack to cool. ■

This recipe was given to me by a friend's grandmother. I used to make these so often that my sister painted a special wooden tool for me that says "Susie's tarts." She has passed away, and I treasure the tool and the memories of the pecan tarts we ate together. —SM

Sarah Gross
Barnegat, New Jersey

Sarah's
Adorable Pie Tarts

Makes 30 tarts

2 (15-count) boxes
  mini phyllo shells
1 (22-ounce) can
  lemon pie filling
1 (21-ounce) can
  cherry pie filling
1 (21-ounce) can
  apple pie filling
4 cups heavy whipping cream
Dash of vanilla extract

Pinch of sugar
Yellow decorating
  sugar, for garnish
10 lemon Skittles, for garnish
Red decorating sugar,
  for garnish
2 tablespoons cinnamon-
  sugar mixture
Honey-roasted almonds,
  chopped, for garnish

Preheat the oven to 350°F. Place the phyllo shells on a baking sheet. Fill 10 shells with the lemon pie filling, 10 with the cherry filling, and 10 with the apple filling. Bake for 5 minutes.

In a large bowl, combine the whipping cream, vanilla, and pinch of sugar and beat until stiff peaks form. Top each tart with a dollop of the whipped cream.

For the lemon tarts, sprinkle the yellow decorating sugar over the top of the whipped cream and top each with a lemon Skittle. For the cherry tarts, sprinkle the red decorating sugar on the top of each one. For the apple tarts, sprinkle the cinnamon-sugar mixture over the top of each and top with the honey-roasted almonds. ∎

The possibilities are endless, and the best part is that these are so quick and easy, you can make them right after dinner. —SG

pies, tarts, cobblers & crisps

Adrienne Massel
Beloit, Wisconsin

Rum–Whipped Cream Pie

Makes one 9-inch pie

1 tablespoon unflavored
  gelatin
1/4 cup cold water
1 cup milk, scalded
6 tablespoons sugar
2 egg whites

1/8 teaspoon salt
3 tablespoons rum
1 cup heavy whipping cream
1 (9-inch) baked pie crust
Grated chocolate, for garnish

In a large bowl, soften the gelatin in the cold water. Stir in the scalded milk and mix well. Add the sugar and stir until both the sugar and gelatin are completely dissolved. Chill until the mixture is nearly set. In a separate bowl, combine the egg whites and salt and beat until stiff. Whip the thickened gelatin until light and spongy. Fold in the egg whites and rum. In another bowl, whip the cream, and then fold into the gelatin mixture. Pour the filling into the pie crust and sprinkle the grated chocolate on top. Chill until firm. ■

I found this in the 1960 edition of *The Best of All Cookbook* and first made it for a family holiday dinner. It became a traditional holiday favorite. I stopped making the pie for a time due to warnings of salmonella in uncooked eggs, but then I became aware of safe, dry, 100 percent egg whites that whip when reconstituted with water. Happily, the pie is once again on our family holiday menu. —AM

Dee Jordan
Riverview, Florida

Peanut Butter Pie

Makes one 9-inch pie

1 cup creamy peanut butter
2 cups confectioners' sugar
1 (9-inch) baked pie
 crust, cooled
2 (3.4-ounce) boxes instant
 vanilla pudding mix

2 3/4 cups plus 1 cup
 cold milk, divided
2 envelopes whipped topping
 mix, such as Dream Whip
1 teaspoon vanilla extract

In a medium bowl, blend together the peanut butter and confectioners' sugar. Spread two-thirds of the mixture onto the bottom and sides of the pie crust. In another bowl, mix the pudding mix and the 2 3/4 cups of the milk according to package instructions. Pour the pudding over the peanut butter filling. Refrigerate for 15 minutes.

Prepare the Dream Whip with the remaining 1 cup of milk and the vanilla according to package directions. Spoon the whipped topping over the pudding, leaving 1 inch of the pudding showing around the edges. Top the whipped topping with the remaining one-third of the peanut butter mixture, lightly pressing it into the whipped topping. Refrigerate until ready to serve. ■

A dear friend gave the recipe to me, and every time I make it, it reminds me of her. All my friends call me the Queen of Cooking, and this pie gave me that reputation! I just don't tell them how simple and easy it is to make. My secret! —DJ

pies, tarts, cobblers & crisps

Chris Morse
Columbia, South Carolina

Easy Pineapple Pie

Makes one 9-inch pie

1 (8-ounce) container
sour cream

1 (8-ounce) can crushed
pineapple with juice

1 (3.4-ounce) box instant
vanilla pudding mix

1 (9-inch) prepared graham
cracker pie crust

1 (8-ounce) container
thawed frozen
whipped topping

In a large bowl, mix together the sour cream, pineapple, and pudding mix. Pour the mixture into the pie crust. Top the pie with the whipped topping and refrigerate until ready to serve. ∎

This is an excellent light dessert! We love it in the summertime, but it is great anytime.—CM

Judi Zito
Miami, Florida

Key Lime Pie

Makes one 9-inch pie

1 (8-ounce) container
thawed frozen
whipped topping
1 (14-ounce) can sweetened
condensed milk

1/4 cup Key lime juice,
preferably freshly squeezed
1 (9-inch) prepared graham
cracker pie crust

In a large bowl, blend the whipped topping, condensed milk, and Key lime juice. Pour the filling into the crust and refrigerate for 30 minutes. ■

Years ago, my mother won a Key lime pie contest in the Florida Keys with this recipe. She entered on the spur of the moment, and this recipe is so quick and easy that she was able to enter in time. She beat several bakers who had made the more traditional version using whipped meringue, much to their chagrin! Later that evening, while out to dinner, she overheard one of the contest competitors at an adjacent table growing that my mom's pie should have been disqualified because it was so simple. —JZ

pies, tarts, cobblers & crisps

Marsha Konken
Sterling, Colorado

Frozen Citrus Pie

Makes one 9-inch pie

1 (6-ounce) can thawed
frozen lemonade
1 pint vanilla ice
cream, softened

1 (8-ounce) container
thawed frozen
whipped topping
1 (9-inch) prepared graham
cracker pie crust

Blend the lemonade and ice cream in a large bowl with a mixer. Stir in the whipped topping. Pour the mixture into the graham cracker crust and place in the freezer for 1 hour. Store leftovers in the freezer. ■

I think I found this recipe in a magazine many years ago. I make it several times in the summer, as it's a cool, refreshing treat and so easy to prepare. —MK

Nina Marquez Johns
Las Vegas, New Mexico

Cupa, Cupa, Cupa Cobbler

Makes 6 servings

1/2 cup butter
1 cup all-purpose flour
1 cup sugar
1 1/2 tablespoons
  baking powder
1/4 teaspoon salt
1/2 teaspoon ground
  cinnamon (optional)

1 cup milk
1 (15-ounce) can cling
  peaches, drained, or
  1 (21-ounce) can
  cherry pie filling
Vanilla ice cream, for serving

Preheat the oven to 350°F. In an 8-inch square glass baking dish, melt the butter for 35 seconds in the microwave.

In a large bowl, mix together all of the dry ingredients. Add the milk and mix until smooth. Pour the dough mixture on top of the butter in the dish. Arrange the peaches on top of the dough so they are evenly spaced. If using pie filling, drop by teaspoonfuls evenly over the dough. Bake for 35 to 40 minutes, until the dough covers the filling and is golden brown. Serve hot with a scoop of ice cream. ■

My mother made this recipe when I was growing up. It was the first dish I learned to make by myself. When my two girls were growing up, they would ask for the cupa, cupa, cupa cobbler, and it later became the first thing they learned to make, too. Now they are grown, and they still make it. It is so easy it has never failed. —NMJ

pies, tarts, cobblers & crisps

Carrie Bachand
Superior, Wisconsin

Autumn Apple Crisp

Makes 8 servings

1 cup plus 1/4 cup
 sugar, divided
1 teaspoon plus 3/4 teaspoon
 ground cinnamon, divided
5 medium apples,
 peeled and sliced
1 cup all-purpose flour
1 teaspoon baking powder

1/2 teaspoon salt
1/2 cup cold butter, cut
 into 1/2-inch cubes
3/4 cup water
Vanilla ice cream or
 cinnamon whipped
 topping, for serving

Preheat the oven to 400°F. Grease an 8-inch square or 9-inch square baking pan. Mix the 1/4 cup of the sugar and 1 teaspoon of the cinnamon in a large bowl. Add the apples and toss to combine. Spread in the prepared pan.

In a small bowl, mix together the flour, baking powder, salt, and the remaining 1 cup of sugar until well combined. Cut in the butter until it forms a crumbly mixture. Sprinkle over the apples and press down slightly. Slowly pour the water over all. Sprinkle the remaining 3/4 teaspoon of cinnamon over the top. Bake, uncovered, for 40 to 45 minutes, until the apples are tender and the topping is golden. Serve warm with ice cream or cinnamon whipped topping. ■

This is comfort-food dessert at its best! A relative staying over for a visit was given her options for something I could make her for breakfast the next morning, and she replied, "Do you have any of that cobbler left?" —CB

Tracie Sayre
San Diego, California

Gluten-Free Apple-Cranberry Crisp

Makes 6 servings

4 cups peeled and
  chopped apples
2 cups fresh or thawed
  frozen cranberries
1/2 cup sugar
1/2 teaspoon ground
  cinnamon

1 cup plus 1 cup gluten-free
  old-fashioned or quick-
  cooking rolled oats, divided
3/4 cup packed brown sugar
1/2 cup butter, melted
1/2 cup chopped
  walnuts or pecans
Ice cream or whipped
  cream, for serving

Preheat the oven to 350°F. Lightly grease an 8-inch square baking dish. In the dish, combine the apples and cranberries. In a small bowl, combine the sugar and cinnamon and sprinkle evenly over the fruit, stirring gently to coat.

Whirl 1 cup of the oats in a food processor or blender to make oat flour. Place 1/3 cup of the oat flour in a large bowl with the brown sugar, the remaining 1 cup of oats, and the melted butter. Mix well. Sprinkle this mixture over the apples and cranberries. Top with the nuts. Bake, uncovered, for 55 minutes to 1 hour, until lightly browned and bubbly. Serve warm with ice cream or whipped cream. ■

This simple but beautiful dessert is elegant enough to serve to guests and easy enough to take to my book club! Fresh cranberries are tart, so plan to serve this with ice cream or whipped cream. —TS

pies, tarts, cobblers & crisps

71

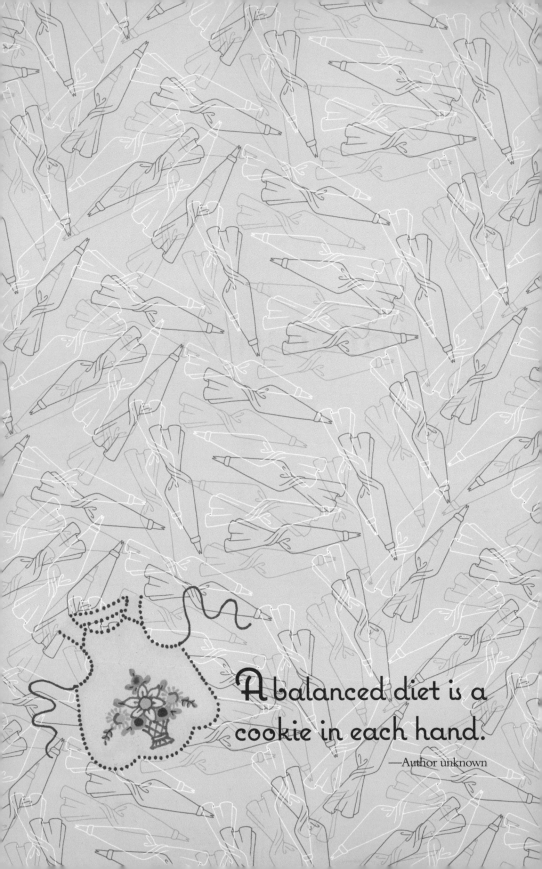

A balanced diet is a cookie in each hand.

—Author unknown

Cookies, Bars & Brownies

Kathy Lowe
Orem, Utah

Cream Wafer Cookies

Makes 24 cookies

1/2 cup butter
1/2 cup margarine
1/2 cup heavy
   whipping cream
2 cups all-purpose flour
Sugar, for sprinkling

Filling
1/4 cup butter, softened
3/4 cup confectioners' sugar
1 egg yolk
1 teaspoon vanilla extract
1 to 4 drops red
   food coloring

Preheat the oven to 350°F. In a large bowl, mix the butter, margarine, cream, and flour well; chill for 30 minutes. Roll out the dough thinly on a floured board. Cut out the dough into 2-inch circles. Place on an ungreased baking sheet and sprinkle lightly with sugar. Bake for 7 to 9 minutes. Let cool.

While the cookies are cooling, make the filling. In a medium bowl, beat together the butter, confectioners' sugar, egg yolk, vanilla, and food coloring until smooth. Frost the bottom of one cookie with the filling and place another cookie on top, bottom side facing the frosting. Repeat with the remaining cookies. ■

This is our special family cookie recipe that we only make once a year to eat on Christmas Eve. It's easy to make and everyone loves them—especially since they know there won't be more made for another year! —KL

Peggy Blanchette
Charlotte, Vermont

Chocolate Chip Crispers

Makes 30 cookies

1/2 cup butter, softened
1 cup sugar
1 egg
1 teaspoon vanilla extract
1 1/4 cups all-purpose flour
1/2 teaspoon baking soda

1/4 teaspoon salt
2 cups crispy rice cereal
1 cup semisweet
   chocolate chips or
   milk chocolate chips

Preheat the oven to 350°F. Grease a baking sheet.

In a large bowl, combine the butter, sugar, egg, and vanilla and mix well. In a separate bowl, mix together the flour, baking soda, and salt. Add the flour mixture to the butter mixture and stir together. Stir in the rice cereal and chocolate chips. Drop by teaspoonfuls onto the baking sheet. Bake for 11 to 12 minutes, until blond in color; they darken a little upon cooling. ■

Whenever we travel to family gatherings out of state, I am expected to bring these cookies. One Thanksgiving many years ago, I showed up with another kind of cookie and was given a timeout on the porch—luckily not for long, as it was cold out there! I have never shown up since without a double batch of these. —PB

cookies, bars & brownies

Jennifer Creecy
Henderson, Tennessee

Toffee-Chocolate Chip Cookies

Makes 36 cookies

1/2 cup salted butter, softened

1 (18.25-ounce) box yellow cake mix

2 eggs

1 teaspoon vanilla extract

1 (8-ounce) bag milk chocolate–covered toffee bits, such as Heath

1 (12-ounce) bag semisweet chocolate chips

1 to 2 tablespoons milk (optional)

Preheat the oven to 350°F. Line a baking sheet with parchment paper. In a large bowl, combine the butter, cake mix, eggs, vanilla, toffee bits, and chocolate chips. Mix until the dough forms; if necessary, add the milk 1 tablespoon at a time to help the dough come together. Roll the dough into balls about 2 tablespoons in size. Place the dough 2 inches apart on the prepared baking sheet. Bake for 12 minutes, or until golden brown. Let the cookies rest on the baking sheet for 1 to 2 minutes before transferring to a wire rack to cool completely. ■

These are the most incredible chocolate chip cookies! Nobody ever believes that they are simply cake-mix cookies. It's almost dangerous to have such an easy recipe for such yummy cookies! —JC

Heidi Woodruff
Coos Bay, Oregon

White Chocolate Chip-Cranberry Cookies

Makes 48 cookies

1/2 cup sugar
1 cup packed light
  brown sugar
1 cup butter, softened
1 teaspoon vanilla extract
2 eggs, beaten
2 1/4 cups all-purpose flour

1 teaspoon baking soda
1/2 teaspoon salt
1 (12-ounce) bag white
  chocolate chips
1/2 cup dried cranberries (or
  thawed frozen, chopped)

Preheat the oven to 375°F. In a large bowl, blend together the sugars, butter, and vanilla until creamy. Mix in the eggs. Gradually add the flour, baking soda, and salt and mix well. Stir in the white chocolate chips and cranberries. Drop by the rounded teaspoonful 2 inches apart on an ungreased baking sheet. Bake for 9 to 11 minutes, until golden brown. ■

We live 15 minutes from the cranberry bogs of the West Coast. Our weather produces some of the best-tasting cranberries. I use them in muffins, cookies, scones, breads, sauce, and, of course, I dry them like Craisins. You can substitute Craisins in any recipe that calls for raisins. They're a delicious addition to coleslaw, too. —HW

cookies, bars & brownies

Karen Peterson
Suamico, Wisconsin

Uncle Joe's
Funeral Cookies

Makes 36 cookies

1 1/4 cups sugar
1 1/4 cups butter
1 1/2 cups all-purpose flour
1/2 teaspoon salt
1 teaspoon baking soda
1/2 teaspoon cream of tartar
1/2 teaspoon vanilla extract

1/2 cup finely
    chopped pecans
2 cups cornflakes cereal,
    finely crushed
Confectioners' sugar,
    for sprinkling

Preheat the oven to 350°F. Line a baking sheet with parchment paper.

In a large bowl, cream together the sugar and butter. In a separate bowl, combine the flour, salt, baking soda, and cream of tartar. Slowly add the dry ingredients to the butter mixture. Mix well. Add the vanilla, pecans, and cornflakes and blend.

Roll the dough into walnut-size balls and place them 3 inches apart on the prepared baking sheet. Dip the bottom of a drinking glass in confectioners' sugar and flatten the balls until thin. Bake for 12 minutes, or until almost light brown on the edges. Let cool slightly and sprinkle with confectioners' sugar before serving. ∎

These were served at my uncle's funeral dinner. The lady who baked them didn't have a name for them, and ever since, we refer to them as Uncle Joe's Funeral Cookies. —KP

Jodi Nance
Kaysville, Utah

Aunt Candi's
Sugar Cookies

Makes 36 cookies

1 cup butter, softened
2 cups sugar
5 eggs
5 cups all-purpose flour
2 teaspoons baking soda
1 teaspoon vanilla extract

Frosting
1 cup butter, softened
1 (8-ounce) package
   cream cheese
4 cups confectioners' sugar

Coarse white sugar
   crystals, for garnish

In a large bowl, beat together the butter, sugar, and eggs. Add the flour, baking soda, and vanilla and mix well. Refrigerate the dough for 2 hours or overnight.

Preheat the oven to 350°F. On a floured surface, roll out the dough 1/4 inch thick and cut out the cookies with a medium cookie cutter. Arrange on an ungreased baking sheet and bake for 10 to 12 minutes, being careful to not overbake. Let cool completely.

In a large bowl, cream together the butter, cream cheese, and confectioners' sugar. With a pastry bag and large star frosting tip, pipe a thick layer of frosting on top of each cookie. Sprinkle with sugar crystals. ■

Every year a local children's hospital raises money by having a "Festival of the Tree." We like to work in the "Sweet Shop." One year we made zillions of these and couldn't keep up with the demand. —JN

cookies, bars & brownies

Sue Dulle
Kansas City, Missouri

Sugar Cookies with Icing

Makes 36 cookies

4 1/2 cups all-purpose flour
1 1/2 teaspoons salt
1 teaspoon baking soda
1 cup butter
1 1/2 cups sugar
3 eggs
1 teaspoon vanilla extract
1/4 teaspoon almond extract

Icing

1/3 cup butter, softened
3 1/2 cups (1 pound)
   confectioners' sugar
1/4 teaspoon salt
1/4 cup milk
1 teaspoon vanilla extract
Food coloring (optional)

In a medium bowl, sift together the flour, salt, and baking soda. In a large bowl, cream together the butter, sugar, eggs, and vanilla and almond extracts until smooth. Slowly add the flour mixture to the butter mixture and mix well. On a large piece of waxed paper dusted with flour, pat the dough into a log shape (about 3 inches in diameter and 10 to 12 inches long), wrap up the log, and chill for at least 1 hour. (I put the logs in plastic bags if storing for a day or two.)

When ready to bake, preheat the oven to 350°F. Cut each roll into thirds; keep the pieces you're not working with in the refrigerator. Using lots of flour, roll out the dough to a scant 1/4-inch thickness. Cut out your desired shapes and arrange on an ungreased baking sheet. (Note: When I use colored sugars instead of icing, I place the cookies on waxed paper, brush with egg white and a couple drops of water beaten well, and then

thickly coat them with the sugar.) Bake for 8 to 10 minutes. Let cool on the pan for a few minutes, then transfer to a wire rack to cool completely.

To make the icing, cream together the butter, sugar, salt, milk and vanilla until smooth and creamy (a bit thicker than yogurt but not as thick as a set pudding). Add drops of milk to thin if necessary. Separate into batches and color with food coloring as desired. Ice the cookies and let set before serving. ■

A friend gave me this recipe because she loved it but thought it was too much work. I have been making these for Christmas since the early 1970s. It took me a year or two to perfect the method. Now my grown sons and their families, my nieces and their families, and dear friends all expect them. Every year I say is my last, but I still bake 40 to 50 dozen cookies a year. —SD

Cheryle Switzer
The Colony, Texas

Cherry-Chocolate-Oatmeal Cookies

Makes 40 cookies

1 cup butter, softened
1 cup sugar
1 cup packed brown sugar
2 eggs
1 teaspoon vanilla extract
2 cups all-purpose flour
1 teaspoon baking soda
1/4 teaspoon baking powder
1 teaspoon salt

1 1/2 teaspoons
   ground cinnamon
1/2 cup chopped
   dried cherries
1/2 cup chopped
   semisweet chocolate
   or chocolate chips
2 3/4 cups quick-
   cooking rolled oats

In a large bowl, cream the butter and both sugars together. Beat the eggs and vanilla together in a cup and add to the mixture. In a smaller bowl, blend the flour, baking soda, baking powder, salt, and cinnamon, then add to the liquid mixture. Stir in the cherries and chocolate, followed by the oats. Cover and chill for 1 hour.

Preheat the oven to 350°F. Grease a baking sheet or line it with parchment paper. Drop the dough by rounded tablespoons onto the baking sheet and bake for about 8 minutes, or until golden brown. ■

These really hit the spot and smell so good while they are cooking—and oatmeal is good for you! —CS

Kimberly McCollum
Pickens, South Carolina

Butter Pecan Cookies

Makes 20 cookies

1 (15.25-ounce) box
   butter pecan cake mix
1/4 cup vegetable oil
1/4 cup water

1 egg
1 cup chopped pecans or
   semisweet chocolate chips

Preheat the oven to 400°F.

In a large bowl, combine all of the ingredients and mix with a mixer on medium speed until smooth and well blended. Drop the dough by rounded tablespoons about 1 inch apart onto an ungreased baking sheet. Bake for 12 to 16 minutes, until golden. ■

This is a family favorite because it is simple and easy to do with my kids. Not only can we enjoy some quality time together baking, but we also can enjoy the yummy results together! —KM

cookies, bars & brownies

Christine Geery
Salt Lake City, Utah

Traditional Sicilian Christmas Cookies

Makes 60 cookies

2 1/2 cups all-purpose flour
1/2 teaspoon baking powder
1/4 cup unsweetened
  cocoa powder, sifted
1 1/2 teaspoons
  ground cinnamon
1/2 cup butter
2 eggs

1 cup sugar
1/4 cup chopped walnuts
  or hazelnuts, toasted

Icing

2 cups confectioners' sugar
3 to 4 tablespoons water

Preheat the oven to 300°F. Spray a baking sheet with nonstick cooking spray.

In a medium bowl, combine the flour, baking powder, cocoa powder, and cinnamon and whisk to blend. In a large bowl, beat the butter, eggs, and sugar until well blended. Add the dry ingredients and blend. Fold in the nuts. Roll the dough into 1 1/4-inch balls. Place the balls 1/2 inch apart on the baking sheet. Bake for 6 to 8 minutes, until the cookies are just set; do not overbake. Let cool on the baking sheet.

To make the icing, place the confectioners' sugar in a small, deep bowl for dipping. Stir in the water 1 tablespoon at a time until it forms a glaze. Drop the cookies in the icing, then remove with a fork, tapping the fork on the side of the bowl to remove excess icing. Place the cookies on waxed paper until dry. Store in an airtight container in the refrigerator, or freeze the cookies between sheets of waxed paper. ■

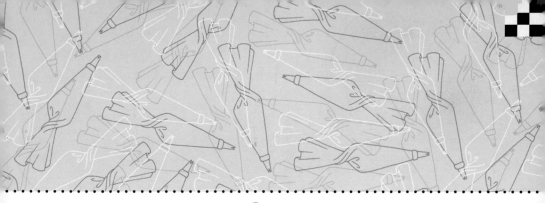

My great-grandparents brought this recipe, with them when they emigrated from Sicily to Canada sometime in the mid-1800s. It has most likely been revised throughout the years, because back in those days they rarely used measurements. One thing is for sure: It wouldn't be Christmas without these cookies. The texture is chewy but not heavy, and they have a rich chocolate flavor, making them the perfect accompaniment for milk, coffee, and tea. —CG

Pamela Newberry
Bellaire, Texas

Mexican Christmas Cookies

Makes 72 cookies

3 cups all-purpose flour
1 teaspoon salt
1 teaspoon ground ginger
1 teaspoon ground
  cinnamon
1 teaspoon ground cloves
6 ounces chopped,
  pitted dates

1 cup chopped pecans
1 cup butter
2 cups sugar
3 eggs, well beaten
1 teaspoon baking soda
3 tablespoons milk

Sift together the flour, salt, ginger, cinnamon, and cloves. Mix in the dates and pecans. In a large bowl, cream the butter. Add the sugar gradually and continue creaming until light and fluffy. Add the eggs and mix well. In a small bowl, dissolve the baking soda in the milk. Mix it into the butter mixture. Gradually add the flour mixture to the butter mixture and blend well. Shape the dough into three rolls about 2 inches in diameter, wrap in waxed paper, and chill thoroughly.

Preheat the oven to 375°F. Line a baking sheet with parchment paper. Slice the dough thinly and place the rounds about 2 inches apart on the baking sheet. Bake for about 10 minutes, or until lightly golden on the edges. ■

This recipe is from my grandma. It was published in many of the Milwaukee Gas Company's Festive Foods cookbooks after my grandma worked in their home-service department in the early 1950s. —PN

Sheri Olson
Coburg, Oregon

Nana O's

Peppernuts

Makes 72 cookies

1 1/2 cups sugar
3/4 cup butter
1 egg
1 cup molasses
1 teaspoon baking
 soda dissolved in 1
 tablespoon hot water
4 1/2 to 5 cups all-
 purpose flour

1 teaspoon ground
 cinnamon
1/2 teaspoon ground ginger
1/2 teaspoon ground cloves
3/4 to 1 teaspoon crushed
 or ground anise seeds
1/2 teaspoon salt
1 cup finely chopped walnuts

In a large bowl, combine all of the ingredients and mix well to form a stiff dough. Refrigerate for several hours or overnight.

Preheat the oven to 275°F.

Roll the dough into a long cylinder and break off pieces the size of a cherry. Roll each piece into a ball and place 2 inches apart on an ungreased baking sheet. Bake for 22 to 23 minutes, until firm and browning on the edges. Let cool completely. Store in an airtight container. These freeze well. ∎

This is a cookie that my husband's mother sent to us every Christmas because it is his favorite. I am the one making them now, since Nana passed away. —SO

cookies, bars & brownies

Lisa Raymaker
Charlotte, North Carolina

Humdingers

Makes 9 squares

1 (8-ounce) package
   chopped dates
1/2 cup butter
1 cup sugar
Pinch of salt

1 teaspoon vanilla extract
2 cups crispy rice cereal
1 cup chopped nuts, such
   as pecans or walnuts
Pinch of confectioners' sugar

Grease a 9-inch square pan.

Cook the dates, butter, sugar, and salt in a medium saucepan over low heat for about 6 minutes, stirring constantly. Remove from the heat and add the vanilla, crispy rice cereal, and nuts. Sprinkle confectioners' sugar in the bottom of the prepared pan, spread the mixture in the pan, and top with more confectioners' sugar. Let cool completely, then cut into squares. ■

This recipe was handed down from my grandmother to my mother, and then to me. My dad loves these, so if we want one we have to get to them before he does! —LR

Jan Thomason
Center Point, Texas

Golly Chews

Makes 48 bars

30 whole graham
  crackers, crushed
2 (14-ounce) cans sweetened
  condensed milk

1 (12-ounce) bag semisweet
  chocolate chips
1 cup chopped pecans,
  toasted (optional)

Preheat the oven to 350°F. Grease a 9 by 13-inch baking dish very well.

Place the graham cracker crumbs in a large bowl. Add the sweetened condensed milk and stir with a strong wooden spoon and a strong arm. Stir in the chocolate chips and nuts. Pour the mixture into the prepared pan. Bake for about 25 minutes, or until the top turns a pretty golden color. You don't want to overcook or undercook, so check them at 20 minutes. Let cool completely, then use a plastic knife to cut into bars. (The bars won't stick to the plastic knife.) ■

My eighty-four-year-old mother got this recipe from our next-door neighbor when I was in elementary school. What to name it? Well, their last name was Golly, so . . . Golly Chews. These bar cookies are my boys' favorite (and all of their friends' favorite, for that matter). —JT

cookies, bars & brownies

89

Amy Dodson
Tulsa, Oklahoma

Grandma Hinshaw's
Date Pinwheels

Makes about 60 cookies

1 cup shortening
1 cup packed brown sugar
1 cup sugar
3 eggs
4 cups all-purpose flour
1/2 teaspoon salt
1/2 teaspoon baking soda

Filling

2 1/4 cups chopped,
   pitted dates
1 cup sugar
1 cup water
Pinch of flour (optional)
1 cup chopped pecans

In a large bowl, combine the shortening, both sugars, eggs, flour, salt, and baking soda and beat well. Chill for 30 minutes.

To make the filling, in a small saucepan over medium heat, combine the dates, sugar, water, and flour (for a smoother consistency). Cook until smooth. Stir in the nuts and set aside to cool.

Roll out one-third of the cookie dough into a rectangle about 8 by 15 inches long and 1/4 inch thick. Spread one-third of the date mixture on top. Roll up into a roll, and repeat until you have three rolls. Wrap with waxed paper and chill the rolls for 1 hour.

Preheat the oven to 350°F. Lightly grease a baking sheet.

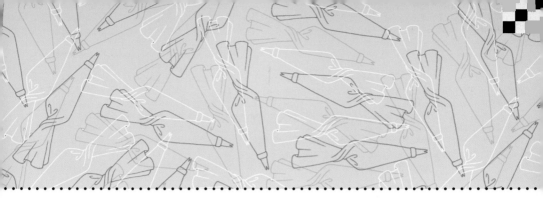

Slice the rolls 1/2 inch thick and place 2 inches apart on the prepared baking sheet. Bake for 10 to 12 minutes, until lightly golden. ■

I grew up in St. Louis in the 1960s. My grandparents took a train from Indianapolis to join our family for the holidays. We loaded into our station wagon and headed downtown to Union Station, anxiously awaiting their arrival. Without fail, when my grandmother stepped off the train she would have a large shirt box tucked under her arm. In this box was a treat that we treasured year after year. Neatly and tightly packed in waxed paper were her delicious Date Pinwheels. This perfect combination of crispy cookie and nutty filling was the taste of the holidays for my family. —AD

cookies, bars & brownies

Glenda Jacobs
Norwalk, California

Raspberry-Walnut Crumble Bars

Makes 24 bars

1 3/4 cups all-purpose flour
1/2 teaspoon kosher salt
1/2 teaspoon ground
   cinnamon
1/4 teaspoon ground
   nutmeg
3/4 cup unsalted
   butter, softened

1 cup sugar
2 large egg yolks
1 teaspoon vanilla extract
2/3 cup seedless
   raspberry jam
1 1/2 cups chopped walnuts

Preheat the oven to 350°F. Spray an 8-inch square baking dish with nonstick cooking spray. Line the pan with a piece of parchment paper, leaving an overhang on two sides. Lightly spray the parchment with cooking spray.

In a medium bowl, whisk together the flour, salt, cinnamon, and nutmeg. In a separate large bowl, beat the butter and sugar with a mixer on medium-high speed until fluffy (2 to 3 minutes). Beat in the egg yolks and vanilla. Decrease the speed to low and gradually add the flour mixture, mixing until just combined. Transfer two-thirds of the dough to the prepared pan and press it into the bottom in an even layer. Spread the jam on top. Sprinkle the nuts over the jam and crumble the remaining dough over the nut topping. Bake for 35 to 45 minutes, until golden brown. Let cool completely in the pan.

Holding both sides of the paper overhang, lift the cake out of the pan, transfer to a cutting board, and cut into 24 rectangles. You can store the bars in an airtight container for up to 5 days. ∎

$\mathcal{I}$ was invited to my first cookie exchange, and it happened to be the day after a Ladies Tea I attended. By the time I got home I was pretty tired, but I needed to make my cookies ahead of time. Our instructions were to bring 3 dozen cookies. I stopped by the market to buy jam. They were out of seedless raspberry, but they had seedless boysenberry and both sugar-free and seedless blackberry, so I bought those. I thought I'd make 1 dozen of each. The day of the exchange I noticed how small the other platters of cookies were compared with mine, and realized I had baked 3 dozen of each flavor! These go great with coffee and are so easy to make. —GI

cookies, bars & brownies

Linda Van Tongeren
Conrad, Montana

Norwegian Almond Bars

Makes 24 bars

First Layer

1 cup butter

1 cup sugar

2 cups all-purpose flour

Second Layer

1 (8-ounce) can
  almond paste

1/2 cup sugar

2 tablespoons butter, softened

2 eggs

Frosting

1/4 cup butter, softened

2 cups confectioners' sugar

2 tablespoons milk

1 teaspoon almond extract

Silvered almonds, for garnish

Preheat the oven to 350°F. Spray a 9 by 13-inch baking dish with nonstick cooking spray.

In a medium bowl, cream together the butter, sugar, and flour. Press the dough into the prepared baking dish. In a separate bowl, combine the second-layer ingredients and blend. Spread the mixture on top of the first layer. Bake for 35 minutes, or until the bars are golden brown. Let cool completely.

While the bars are cooling, make the frosting. In a medium bowl with a mixer, beat together the butter, confectioners' sugar, milk, and almond extract on medium speed until creamy. Spread the frosting on the bars. Garnish with the almonds. Slice and serve. ■

These are very good bars! —LVT

Patricia Cooper
Hemet, California

Irene's Toffee Bars

Makes 50 squares

1 cup packed brown sugar	2 cups all-purpose flour
1/2 cup butter	1 (3-ounce) chocolate
1 egg	bar, broken into pieces
1 teaspoon vanilla extract	Sprinkles, for garnish

Preheat the oven to 350°F. Grease a 9 by 13-inch jelly roll pan.

In a large bowl, cream together the sugar and butter until smooth. Add the egg and vanilla and mix thoroughly. Add the flour and blend well. Press the dough into the prepared pan. Bake for 18 to 20 minutes.

Remove the pan from the oven. Place the chocolate pieces on top of the dough while still hot and let stand for 3 to 5 minutes. Spread the melting chocolate across the cookie, leaving 1/4 inch of edge showing. Top with sprinkles. Refrigerate until the chocolate is set, then cut the bars into 2-inch squares. ■

My parents married on April 5, 1952. My father was in the Air Force and was sent to Korea. My mother baked these cookies because she could mail them to Daddy and they would arrive in delicious shape. I have mailed them to my brother in Iraq. My mother and father have since passed on, but the smell and taste of this cookie make for a memorable treat for my siblings and me. —PC

cookies, bars & brownies

Kathren Martinez
Simi Valley, California

Iced Buttery Almond-Toffee Blondies

Makes 24 brownies

1 1/2 cups butter
2 1/4 cups all-purpose flour
1 1/2 teaspoons
  baking powder
1 teaspoon salt
2 cups packed brown sugar
1/2 cup sugar
3 eggs
1 1/2 teaspoons
  vanilla extract
1 teaspoon almond extract
1 cup chopped almonds
1 cup toffee bits

Frosting

1 (8-ounce) package
  cream cheese, softened
1 cup white chocolate chips
1 tablespoon heavy
  whipping cream
2 cups confectioners' sugar
1 teaspoon almond extract
1/4 cup sliced almonds
  (optional)

Preheat the oven to 350°F. Grease and flour a 9 by 13-inch baking dish.

Place the butter in a saucepan over medium heat and cook, stirring often, until golden brown. Remove from the heat and let cool.

In a large bowl, whisk together the flour, baking powder, and salt. In a separate large bowl with a mixer, beat together the browned butter and sugars until combined. Add the eggs one

96

at a time. Beat on medium speed for 3 minutes. Add the vanilla and almond extracts. Add the flour mixture, almonds, and toffee bits and mix thoroughly. Pour into the prepared pan. Bake for 40 to 45 minutes, until a toothpick inserted in the center comes out clean. Remove from the oven and let cool completely on a wire rack.

To make the frosting, place the cream cheese in the bowl of the mixer and beat on medium speed to soften. Place the white chocolate chips and cream in a medium microwave-safe bowl and microwave at 30-second intervals until melted. Stir together. Add the melted chocolate to the cream cheese and mix just until blended. Beat in the confectioners' sugar and almond extract until smooth. Spread over the cooled blondies and garnish with sliced almonds, if desired. Refrigerate for 30 minutes to 1 hour. Cut into bars. ∎

This recipe was created as an entry for our local county fair, the Ventura County Fair. I had lots of people try it before the entry, and everyone loved it! It took a blue ribbon, and now it is the dessert everyone asks me to make for them. —KM

cookies, bars & brownies

Vanessa Bogaty
St. Louis, Missouri

Coconut-Pecan Bars

Makes 24 bars

Crust
1 1/2 cups all-purpose flour
3/4 cup confectioners' sugar
3/4 cup butter, softened

Filling
1/4 cup butter, melted
1 1/2 cups packed
   dark brown sugar
3 eggs

3 tablespoons all-
   purpose flour
3/4 teaspoon salt
3/4 teaspoon baking soda
1 teaspoon vanilla extract
3/4 cup coarsely chopped
   pecans, toasted
3/4 cup sweetened
   shredded coconut

Preheat the oven to 325°F. Grease a 9 by 13-inch baking dish.

To make the crust, place the flour, confectioners' sugar, and butter in the bowl of a mixer and mix on medium speed until fully incorporated. The mixture will be crumbly. Evenly press this mixture into the pan. Bake on the middle rack for 10 to 15 minutes, until the crust is golden brown. Remove from the oven and let cool. Leave the oven on.

To make the filling, combine the butter and sugar and mix until fully incorporated. Add the eggs one at a time, mixing well after each addition. Add the flour, salt, baking soda, and vanilla. Stir in the nuts and coconut. Spread the filling over the crust and bake for 20 to 30 minutes, until set. The bars will be a bit gooey but will set like a pecan pie when done. Let the bars cool in the pan for about 10 minutes. Run a knife around the edges of the pan to loosen, then let cool completely. Cut into bars. ■

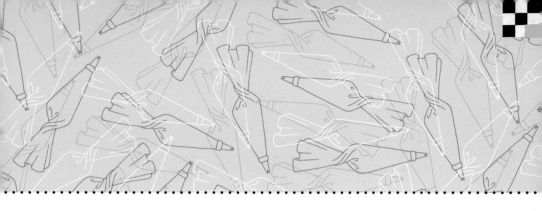

Cookies are my favorite food group, and this is my favorite bar cookie. I've been baking it for almost thirty years and have changed the recipe over the years. As you make it, change what you want to do it your way. I suggest no substitutions for the butter, though. Some things just can't be changed. —VB

cookies, bars & brownies

Fran Rice
Lincoln, California

Pumpkin Dessert Squares

Makes 12 squares

Crust

1 (15.25-ounce) box
spice cake mix
1/2 cup finely
chopped pecans
1/2 teaspoon salt
1/4 teaspoon baking soda
3/4 cup plus 2 tablespoons
vegetable oil

Filling

1 (15-ounce) can pumpkin
puree (not pie filling)
3/4 cup sugar
1 (12-ounce) can
evaporated milk

2 teaspoons ground
cinnamon
3/4 teaspoon ground ginger
1/4 teaspoon ground cloves
2 eggs

Topping

Fresh whipped cream
(with a pinch of ground
nutmeg added, if desired)
Chopped pecans or
walnuts (optional)
Chocolate sprinkles
(optional)

Preheat the oven to 350°F. Grease a 9 by 13-inch baking dish.

To make the crust, combine the cake mix, pecans, salt, baking soda, and oil in a large bowl and blend. Press the crust evenly into the prepared pan. Bake for 20 minutes, or until the crust is slightly brown.

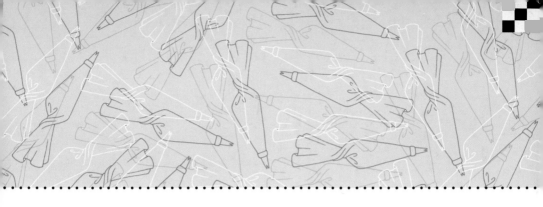

While the crust is baking, make the pumpkin filling. In a medium bowl, combine all of the filling ingredients and blend until smooth. Remove the crust from the oven and pour the filling over it. Bake for 30 minutes more, or until the center is firm. Let cool completely.

Spread the whipped cream over the pumpkin filling. Garnish with the pecans and/or chocolate sprinkles. Refrigerate any leftovers. ■

This is a great deviation from pumpkin pie. It has the traditional taste with a unique and delectable crust! —FR

Susan Ego
Corte Madera, California

Pumpkin Crunch Bars

Makes 8 large bars

1 (13-ounce) can pumpkin puree (not pie filling)
1 (12-ounce) can evaporated milk
1 cup sugar
3 eggs
1 teaspoon ground cinnamon

1 (15.25-ounce) box yellow cake mix
1 cup chopped walnuts
1 cup butter, melted
Vanilla ice cream, whipped cream, or confectioners' sugar, for serving

Preheat the oven to 350°F. Grease a 9 by 13-inch baking dish and line it with parchment paper.

In a large bowl combine the pumpkin, evaporated milk, sugar, eggs, and cinnamon and mix well. Pour into the prepared pan. Sprinkle half of the dry cake mix over the batter. Sprinkle with the nuts and the remaining cake mix. Pour the melted butter over the top. Bake for 50 minutes to 1 hour, until a toothpick inserted in the center comes out clean. Let cool completely.

Use a knife to loosen the edges from the pan. Invert onto a large platter or cutting board and cut into 8 bars. To serve, top with vanilla ice cream or whipped cream, or simply dust with confectioners' sugar. ■

I make this every holiday for dessert. My four kids love it and will not touch regular pumpkin pie ever again. It has always been a crowd-pleaser whenever we have it. —SE

JoLisa Hoover
Cedar Park, Texas

Ms. JoLisa's
Texas Brownies

Makes 24 brownies

1 teaspoon salt
1 teaspoon baking powder
1 1/2 cups all-purpose flour
1 cup vegetable oil
2 cups sugar

3/8 to 1/2 cup unsweetened
    cocoa powder
1 tablespoon light corn syrup
1 teaspoon vanilla extract
4 eggs, lightly beaten
2 cups milk chocolate chips

Preheat the oven to 350°F. Spray a 7 by 11-inch baking pan with nonstick cooking spray.

Combine the salt, baking powder, flour, oil, sugar, cocoa powder, corn syrup, vanilla, and eggs in a large bowl and mix by hand with a wooden spoon. Pour the batter into the prepared pan. Bake for 25 to 30 minutes, until a toothpick inserted in the center comes out clean. Sprinkle with the chocolate chips while still warm. Let cool completely, then cut into squares. ∎

As an avid chocolate lover, I started experimenting with brownie recipes when I was ten years old, and I eventually perfected a version to achieve the maximum amount of chocolate. I called them Texas Brownies because they hold a Texas-size amount of chocolate. These have been a favorite of my fellow teachers, students, and my children's choir and Sunday school friends. I once came home to find a message begging for brownies. —JH

cookies, bars & brownies

Patricia Prettyman
Portland, Oregon

Chocolate Lover's Brownies

Makes 28 brownies

2 (1-ounce) semisweet
  baking chocolate
  squares, chopped
1 cup salted butter, softened
3 tablespoons chocolate-
  hazelnut spread,
  such as Nutella
1 teaspoon instant
  coffee granules
1 (12-ounce) bag mini
  semisweet chocolate chips

4 eggs, at room temperature
2 cups sugar
1/4 cup canola oil
1 teaspoon sea salt
3 tablespoons unsweetened
  cocoa powder
2 teaspoons vanilla extract
2 cups all-purpose flour
1/4 teaspoon baking soda
1/2 teaspoon baking powder
1 cup chopped walnuts

Preheat the oven to 350°F. Spray 28 muffin cups with nonstick cooking spray.

In the top of a double boiler over medium-low heat or in a heatproof glass bowl set over a saucepan of simmering water, combine the chopped chocolate, butter, hazelnut spread, instant coffee, and 1/2 cup of the mini chocolate chips. Stir until all ingredients are melted and combined. Set aside to cool.

In a large bowl with a mixer, beat the eggs on medium speed until fluffy, about 4 minutes. Slowly add the sugar and mix on medium speed for 3 minutes, scraping the sides of the bowl. The mixture should be fluffy. Add the oil, sea salt, cocoa powder, and vanilla and mix till incorporated. In a separate large bowl, whisk together the flour, baking soda, and baking powder.

Add half of the flour mixture to the egg mixture and blend, alternating with the cooled melted chocolate mixture until all is combined. Fold in 1/2 cup of the mini chocolate chips and the walnuts.

Use a 2-inch cookie scoop to divide the batter among the muffin cups. Bake for 20 minutes, or until a toothpick inserted in the center comes out fairly clean. A little chocolate on the toothpick is normal because of the chocolate chips. While hot, use a knife to loosen and release the brownies and transfer them to a wire rack. Carefully sprinkle some of the remaining chocolate chips on top of each brownie while still warm. Let cool completely. Store the brownies in a single layer in an airtight container. ■

My brother-in-law is a complete chocoholic, so one Christmas I decided to create a brownie recipe with four types of chocolate, and it was a complete hit with him and everyone else. They are moist inside but have the crunchy edges that make a brownie a brownie. Adding mini chocolate chips on top as they are cooling creates a sweet, creamy topping instead of frosting. —PP

cookies, bars & brownies

Lisa Raymaker
Charlotte, North Carolina

Iced Brownies

Makes 12 brownies

2 cups sugar

2 cups all-purpose flour

4 eggs

5 tablespoons unsweetened
cocoa powder

1 cup butter, melted

1 1/2 cups chopped
pecans (optional)

Frosting

1/4 cup butter, melted

2 tablespoons unsweetened
cocoa powder

1 (16-ounce) package
confectioners' sugar

1 teaspoon vanilla extract

Dash of milk

1 cup chopped pecans
(optional)

Preheat the oven to 350°F. Grease a 9 by 13-inch baking dish.

In a large bowl, mix together the sugar, flour, eggs, cocoa powder, melted butter, and pecans, if using. Pour the batter into the prepared pan. Bake for 30 minutes, or until a toothpick inserted in the center comes out clean. Let cool completely.

To make the frosting, beat together the melted butter, cocoa powder, confectioners' sugar, and vanilla in a large bowl with a mixer on medium speed. Add a little milk, if necessary, to achieve a spreadable consistency. Stir in the chopped pecans, if using. Spread the icing on the cooled brownies. Cut into squares. ∎

This recipe has been handed down from my grandmother to my mother to me. Baking them brings back all kinds of wonderful memories! —LR

Bonnie Leatherman
Muskogee, Oklahoma

Toffee Brownies

Makes 24 brownies

2 (8-ounce) bags milk
    chocolate–toffee bits
1 (10.5-ounce) box chewy
    fudge brownie mix
2 eggs
1/4 cup water

1/2 cup vegetable oil
2 teaspoons instant
    coffee granules
1 teaspoon vanilla extract
1/2 teaspoon butter
    flavoring

Preheat the oven to 325°F. Generously spray a 9 by 13-inch glass baking dish with nonstick cooking spray. Evenly sprinkle the toffee bits over the bottom of the dish.

In a large bowl, stir together the brownie mix, eggs, water, oil, coffee granules, vanilla, and butter flavoring. Pour over the toffee bits and spread to the edges of the dish. Bake for 25 to 30 minutes, until a toothpick inserted in the center comes out clean. Cool completely.

When cool, cut with a plastic knife to prevent ragged edges. The first piece may be difficult to get out, but the cook gets to eat it! ■

The magnificent Tivoli Inn in Broken Arrow, Oklahoma, serves tiny, delicious brownie bites. While trying to replicate their recipe, I came up with this. While it's different from theirs, it's delicious, too! —BL

cookies, bars & brownies

107

After eating chocolate
you feel godlike, as though
you can conquer enemies,
lead armies, entice lovers.

—Emily Luchetti

Candies & Fudge

Lissa Coulter
Garner, North Carolina

Totally Addicting
Chocolate-Almond
Toffee

Makes 12 cups

1 1/2 to 2 cups almond meal (store bought, or made by finely grinding raw unsalted almonds in a blender)

1 (12-ounce) bag mini semisweet chocolate chips
2 cups butter
2 cups sugar

Line a 10 by 15-inch jelly roll pan with aluminum foil. Grease the foil. (You can use a larger baking sheet and only cover 10 by 15 inches of it, but do not use a breakable container.) Spread half the almond meal across the foil, then repeat with half the chocolate chips; set aside. Place a couple of ounces of water in a small bowl or cup. Set it, along with a small spoon, next to the stove.

In a large saucepan, melt butter and sugar over medium heat. Stir continually, being careful to really get to the bottom and "corners" of the pan. The mixture will turn from creamy yellow to beige, and ultimately to a medium brown. After about 20 minutes, the mixture will also develop a nutty aroma. Dip the teaspoon in the toffee mixture and then into your cup of water. If it immediately becomes crunchy as the water cools it, it's ready to remove from the heat. If it's still a bit chewy, keep stirring until it tests done. (If you're making it for people who normally shy away from the crunchiness of typical toffees, you can consider it done when there's just a hint of chewiness left.)

Pour the mixture onto the baking sheet on top of the nuts and chocolate chips. Spread the remaining chips over the toffee, then repeat with the remaining nuts. Cover with a sheet of greased foil. Let cool. When cool, with the foil still covering it, use a hammer to break the toffee into pieces. ■

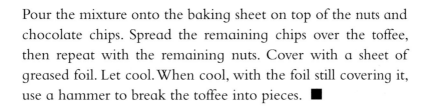

I received the original version of this recipe from a colleague, but I have revised it over the years to make it even more delicious and simpler to make. It has been my favorite holiday treat recipe for at least a dozen years. It travels well and is always *highly* anticipated by friends near and far! I warn people before they try it that my toffee can be very addicting but that I will not give them the recipe. —LC

candies & fudge

Beverly Letsche
St. Lawrence, South Dakota

World's Easiest Peanut Brittle

Makes 6 to 8 cups

Butter, for the pan
1 cup sugar
1/2 cup light corn syrup
Pinch of kosher salt

1 cup unsalted peanuts
1 teaspoon salted butter
1 teaspoon vanilla extract
1 teaspoon baking soda

Line a baking sheet with aluminum foil and butter it well. Combine the sugar, corn syrup, and salt in a 2-quart microwave-safe glass bowl or pan. Microwave on high power for 2 minutes. Stir in the peanuts. Microwave for 2 minutes more. Stir, then microwave for 3 minutes. Stir in the butter and vanilla. Microwave for 1 minute. Stir in the baking soda.

Spread the mixture evenly on the baking sheet. Let cool completely, then break into pieces. Store in a tightly sealed container. ∎

I received this recipe from a friend years ago and tweaked it until I liked the results. It is fast, easy, and reliable. It is greeted with great enthusiasm at family gatherings, and the guys like it best when they are each given a whole batch of their very own as a Christmas present. —BL

Bonnie Eaker
Seminole, Florida

Easy Cookie Truffles

Makes 48 truffles

1 pound semisweet
chocolate, chopped,
or 1 pound semisweet
chocolate chips
1 (8-ounce) package
cream cheese, softened

1 (18-ounce) package
crème-filled chocolate
sandwich cookies
(such as Oreos), finely
crushed (about 4 1/4
cups total), divided

Line a baking sheet with waxed paper. Place the chocolate in a large microwave-safe bowl. Microwave on high power for 2 1/2 minutes, or until completely melted, stirring every 30 seconds. In a large bowl, mix the cream cheese and the 3 cups of the cookie crumbs well. Shape into forty-eight 1-inch balls. Dip in the melted chocolate and place on the prepared pan. (It helps to place a few balls in the chocolate at a time and use two forks to lift each, letting the excess chocolate drip off.) While the chocolate is still soft, sprinkle with the remaining 1 1/2 cups of cookie crumbs. Refrigerate for 1 hour, or until firm. Refrigerate leftovers in a tightly sealed container. ■

These are so simple and can be made with flavored Oreos (such as mint or peanut butter) and covered in white, milk, or dark chocolate. They are fun to make and are just enough with a cup of coffee. I love to pack them in small containers, add a colorful bow and gift tag, and give them as holiday or hostess gifts. —BE

candies & fudge

Denise Rounds
Tulsa, Oklahoma

Gladys's
Baked Fudge

Makes 15 servings

2 cups sugar
1/2 cup all-purpose flour
1/2 cup unsweetened
  cocoa powder

4 eggs
1 cup butter, melted
2 teaspoons vanilla extract
1 cup chopped pecans

Preheat the oven to 325°F.

In a medium bowl, whisk together the sugar, flour, and cocoa. In a large bowl, with a mixer on medium speed, beat the eggs. Add the flour mixture and blend thoroughly. While mixing, slowly pour in the melted butter, followed by the vanilla. Stir in the nuts. Pour into an ungreased 9 by 13-inch baking dish. Set the pan in a larger pan and pour hot water into the larger pan to come partway up the sides of the 9 by 13-inch pan. Bake for 45 minutes, or until a knife inserted in the center comes out clean. Let cool before cutting into squares. ■

My grandmother got this recipe from a Tulsa restaurant in the 1950s. The cook who shared it was named Gladys, as was my grandmother. We have passed this down through four generations. It makes delightful parfaits layered with vanilla bean ice cream and a drizzle of crème de menthe syrup and topped with freshly whipped cream. I've halved the recipe in a pinch using a 9-inch baking pan. —DR

Alexa Anderson
Maryland Heights, Missouri

Mamie's Fudge

Makes 16 servings

2 cups sugar
1 cup milk
2 (1-ounce) squares
   unsweetened Baker's
   chocolate, chopped

2 teaspoons vanilla extract
1 1/2 tablespoons butter

Grease a 9 by 13-inch baking dish. Place a small, clear cup of cold water next to the stovetop. Combine the sugar and milk in a large saucepan over medium heat. Add the chocolate and bring to a rolling boil, stirring. Decrease the heat to a simmer and continue cooking for 20 to 25 minutes, until you can form a soft ball by dropping a small amount of fudge liquid into the cup of cold water. Once a soft ball forms, remove the pan from the heat. Stir in the vanilla and butter and beat with a spoon for about 15 minutes. The fudge should be thick enough to pour when a drizzle of it stays on top and doesn't sink into the rest. Pour the fudge into the prepared pan. Let cool, then cut into squares. ■

I remember as a child watching my mother make this fudge. I would sit at the kitchen table while she beat this dark liquid that smelled so good, checked to see if it was ready to pour, then beat some more. My mouth watered the whole time, and it seemed to take forever. I wondered if it was really worth all the effort she put into it. Believe me, it was, because she made it with love. —AA

candies & fudge

Kimberly Worley
Gretna, Virginia

Fruit Balls

Makes 12 fruit balls

1/2 cup butter
1 cup sugar
1 egg, beaten
8 to 10 ounces
  chopped dates
1 cup candied cherries,
  chopped

1 cup finely chopped pecans
1 teaspoon vanilla extract
2 1/2 cups crispy rice cereal
1 (14-ounce) bag sweetened
  shredded coconut

Melt the butter in a large skillet over medium-low heat. Add the sugar and beaten egg and cook, stirring, until thickened. Mix in the dates, cherries, pecans, and vanilla. Add the crispy rice cereal and mix well. Let cool slightly, then form into 12 balls. Roll in the shredded coconut. Store in an airtight container between layers of waxed paper. These will keep in the refrigerator for about 1 month. ■

When I was a little girl, I would go to my Grandma Alice's and "help" her make goodies for the holidays, and this was my favorite. What memories! For as long as I can remember, it was a tradition to have these placed in a pretty tin and served to family and friends when they stopped by over the holidays. What a great gift to give in a Mary Engelbreit tin! —KW

Alexa Anderson
Maryland Heights, Missouri

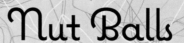

Nut Balls

Makes 48 nut balls

2 1/2 cups all-purpose flour
1/2 cup confectioners' sugar,
  plus more for rolling
1/4 teaspoon salt

2 cups chopped pecans
1 1/2 teaspoons
  vanilla extract
1 cup butter, softened

Preheat the oven to 300°F. Grease a baking sheet.

In a large bowl, mix together the flour, confectioners' sugar, salt, and pecans. Stir in the vanilla. Add the butter and knead with your hands to form a large ball. Shape the dough into 1-inch balls and place them on the prepared baking sheet.

Bake for 45 minutes. Let cool slightly, then roll in confectioners' sugar while still warm. Store in an airtight container between layers of waxed paper. ■

This recipe has been passed down from my mother. She would bake these at Christmastime, and the kitchen would smell of pecans, which I love. This is my sister's favorite cookie, and if I didn't make a batch especially for her every year my name would be mud. My son loves these, too, and will steal some batter before I can get the cookies into the oven. —AA

candies & fudge

Shann Palmer
Richmond, Virginia

Mamaw's
Date Rolls

Makes 45 date rolls

2 pounds dates, pitted
2 pounds nuts, chopped
(such as almonds,
pecans, or walnuts)

2 pounds finely
shredded coconut
45 whole nuts (such as
almonds, pecans, or
walnuts), for garnish

Set aside a small bowl of ice water. Use scissors to cut the dates into small pieces. When the scissors get sticky, dip them in the ice water and wipe off. Use a rolling pin to crush the 2 pounds of nuts. Reserve one-quarter of the crushed nuts and one-quarter of the shredded coconut.

Line two baking sheets with waxed paper. In a large bowl, mix the dates, the remaining three-quarters of the crushed nuts, and the remaining three-quarters of the coconut. Blend well. Roll into balls about the diameter of a quarter, dipping your hands into the ice water when they get too sticky. Mix the reserved crushed nuts and coconut in a bowl. Roll the balls in the nut-coconut mixture to coat. Place the balls on the prepared baking sheets. Flatten each ball just a little and press a whole nut into the top. The balls will keep for about 1 week when stored between layers of waxed paper in an airtight container in the refrigerator. ■

When I was a little girl in Houston, Texas, my grandmother Clara Argen Tyler would cook for weeks leading up to the holidays. In her spacious country kitchen, we (mostly she) mixed the ingredients until they were a sticky mess, and then it was completely up to me to roll them into balls. I probably rolled thousands before I moved away for college! I give them to my choir in sealed bags in Mary Engelbreit boxes each year. I know at least one soprano who makes sure to sing each December to get her date rolls! You can also add things such as orange zest, cocoa powder, vanilla, and cinnamon, as desired. —SP

candies & fudge

Resa Bridges
Glen Carbon, Illinois

Grandma O'Barâ's
Date Roll

Makes 8 servings

1 (8-ounce) package
  whole dates
12 large marshmallows
16 whole graham crackers

1/2 cup pecan pieces
1/4 cup milk
Whipped cream, for serving

Use scissors to cut the dates and marshmallows into small pieces. (When cutting the dates, it may help to dip the scissors in a bowl of ice water and wipe off as necessary.) Place them in a large bowl. Crush the graham crackers and place half the crumbs in the bowl. (Set aside the other half for rolling.) Add the pecans and milk to the bowl and stir until everything comes together. Shape into one large log about 4 inches long (or two small logs) and roll in the reserved graham cracker crumbs. Wrap the log(s) in waxed paper and refrigerate for at least 1 hour, or until set. Cut into 1/2-inch-thick slices and serve with whipped cream. ■

My mom made date rolls every year. It just wasn't Christmas without Grandma's date rolls. It brings back lots of good holiday memories with family. —RB

Connie Graybill
Louisville, Kentucky

Yummy Potato Candy

Makes 30 candies

1 medium Yukon
  Gold potato

2 (16-ounce) packages
  confectioners' sugar
1 cup smooth peanut butter

Boil the potato until tender and well done. Peel and mash until very smooth. You should have about 1/2 cup. Begin to add the confectioners' sugar a little at a time and mix very well. At first, it will be liquidy. Continue to add sugar and mix until it forms a stiff dough that is easy to handle and shape into a ball. You will need several cups of sugar to achieve the right consistency. Spread more confectioners' sugar on a work surface and knead and roll out the dough to about 1/4 inch thick, using sugar as you would flour to keep it from sticking to the rolling pin.

Spread the top side of the dough round with peanut butter. Gently roll into a log. Wrap the log in waxed paper and refrigerate for about 1 hour. Unwrap the log and cut it into 1/4- to 1/2-inch slices. Store in an airtight container between layers of waxed paper. ■

We have made this in our family for many years. It is a kid-friendly recipe, and it only uses three items, so it is easy on the budget. It fascinates people because they don't believe that there really is potato in the recipe. You won't believe how pretty they are and how wonderful they taste! —CG

candies & fudge

121

Deb Kozel
Des Moines, Iowa

Dorothy's
Divinity

Makes 30 candies

3 cups sugar
2/3 cup water
1/2 cup light corn syrup

3 egg whites
1 teaspoon vanilla extract

Line a baking sheet with waxed paper. In a large, heavy skillet over medium-high heat, combine the sugar, water, and corn syrup and bring to a boil. Cook, but do not stir, until it reaches 250°F on a candy thermometer.

While the sugar mixture is cooking, beat the egg whites until very stiff in a large bowl with a mixer on medium speed. Check the syrup mixture. At 250°F it should spin a ribbon when you lift a little from the pan. Slowly pour the syrup mixture over the egg whites. Add the vanilla and beat until the mixture holds peaks. Spoon bite-size pieces onto waxed paper to cool. Once set, transfer the candies to an airtight container. ■

The good news is that my mom, Dorothy, was a great cook. She would try a recipe and change it to suit her own taste. The bad news is that she *never* had recipes written down. She has passed on, and I make her divinity every Christmas as a reminder that her homemade candy is the best. She would add chopped nuts for flavor variations or flavored gelatin for different colors. —DK

Angela Clark
St. Louis, Missouri

Caramels

Makes 2 1/2 pounds

1 cup butter, plus more
  for coating the dish
2 1/4 cups packed
  brown sugar
Pinch of salt

1 cup light corn syrup
1 (14-ounce) can sweetened
  condensed milk
1 teaspoon vanilla extract

Generously butter a 9-inch square baking pan. In a large saucepan over medium heat, melt the 1 cup of butter. Add the brown sugar and salt and stir thoroughly. Stir in the corn syrup. Gradually add the sweetened condensed milk, stirring constantly. Cook and stir over medium heat until the mixture reaches 245°F on a candy thermometer (the firm-ball stage). The mixture will be at an even boil. Remove from the heat and stir in the vanilla. Pour the mixture into the prepared pan and let cool completely. Cut into squares and wrap each individually with waxed paper. ∎

These are a big hit with family and friends around the holidays. I've even made them as salted caramels for my foodie friends (just press a bit of coarse sea salt on top). All you need is a candy thermometer and a little patience and you're in business. —AC

candies & fudge

Part of the secret of success in
life is to eat what you like and
let the food fight it out inside.

—Mark Twain

Breakfast Sweets & Breads

Lynda Hart
Bluffdale, Utah

Aebleskivers
(Danish Pancake Balls)

Makes 7 pancake balls

2 eggs
2 cups buttermilk
3 tablespoons unsalted
   butter, melted plus
   more for the pan
2 cups all-purpose flour
2 tablespoons sugar
2 teaspoons baking powder
1/2 teaspoon salt

1/4 teaspoon baking soda
Confectioners' sugar
   or cinnamon sugar,
   for dusting
Your favorite toppings,
   such as jam, applesauce,
   chocolate chips, berries,
   or apple or pineapple
   chunks, for serving

Place the aebleskiver pan on the stovetop over medium heat. Separate the egg yolks from the whites and beat the egg whites until stiff. In a separate bowl, combine the egg yolks, buttermilk, butter, flour, sugar, baking powder, salt, and baking soda and beat until smooth. Use a spatula to fold in the egg whites. Add a little melted butter to each cup of the pan. Fill each cup to about 1/4 inch from the top with batter. When the edges begin to bubble, use the tip of a kitchen skewer or chopstick to poke the edge of the batter as it is cooking and to pull up on one side so that the uncooked batter spreads down into the pan and continues to cook. (This may take a little practice, but before long you'll be turning them like a Dane!) Continue turning until each is in the shape of a ball. You may need to add a little more butter as you start each new batch.

(You may wish to place a few chocolate chips, apple or pineapple chunks, or berries in the middle of the batter after the first turn. Press them in until completely covered by batter. Do not add the inside fillings to the batter after the first turn, as it will cause the batter to stick to the pan.)

Dust with confectioners' sugar or cinnamon sugar and serve with your favorite toppings. ■

One of my favorite Christmas memories is going to my grandmother's house and having her bring in her big tin lined with waxed paper. As she opened the lid, I'd get the first whiff of the delectable *aebleskivers* dusted with confectioners' sugar or cinnamon sugar. Grandma made them at other times of the year, but they were especially good at Christmastime. My grandchildren love this special treat when we have sleepovers.

Aebleskivers require a special cast-iron pan with seven rounded indentations. The pans are available online or at kitchen specialty stores. —LH

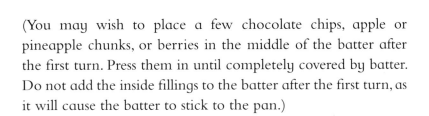

breakfast sweets & breads

Tracy Schaffer
Portland, Oregon

Truffins
(Tracy's Muffins)

Makes 60 muffins

1 (17.7-ounce) box
  bran buds
4 cups buttermilk
2 cups water
5 cups all-purpose flour

3 cups sugar
1 1/2 teaspoons salt
5 teaspoons baking soda
1 1/2 cups butter, melted
4 eggs

In a large bowl, soak the bran buds overnight in the buttermilk and water.

Preheat the oven to 400°F. Grease or line muffin pans with paper liners. Add the flour, sugar, salt, baking soda, butter, and eggs to the bran mixture and stir to combine. Divide the batter among the prepared pans and bake for 18 to 20 minutes, until golden and a toothpick inserted in the center of a muffin comes out clean. ■

I received this recipe from a friend's mother, Colleen Patterson. She always had muffins baking. When I moved away from my family for the first time, I became good friends with my neighbors, a single mom and her two young sons. I made these muffins often! After awhile, the boys called them "Truffins." —TS

Joyce Ingalls
North Hollywood, California

Magic Muffins
from the Pumpkin Patch

Makes 12 muffins

3 tablespoons sugar
1 teaspoon ground
   cinnamon
1 cup vanilla ice cream

1 cup pumpkin puree
   (not pie filling)
1/2 teaspoon vanilla extract
2 cups buttermilk biscuit mix

Preheat the oven to 400°F. Stir together the sugar and cinnamon and set aside. Place paper liners in a 12-cup muffin pan and lightly spray the liners with nonstick cooking spray.

Place the ice cream in a large mixing bowl and stir with a fork until smooth and melted, about 5 minutes. It should be about the consistency of whipping cream. Add the pumpkin puree and vanilla and stir until no streaks remain. Add the baking mix and stir just enough to moisten. Do not overmix.

Fill each muffin cup half full of batter. Sprinkle 1/2 teaspoon of the cinnamon sugar over the batter. Spoon the remaining batter into the muffin cups until each is filled about two-thirds full. Sprinkle the tops with the remaining cinnamon sugar. Bake for 18 to 20 minutes, until a toothpick inserted in the center of a muffin comes out clean. Transfer to a wire rack to cool for about 10 minutes. ■

One morning, my sons Will and Steve said they needed to bring cupcakes to school. That's how these muffins came to be. Steve called them "Magic Muffins," and Will said they tasted like they just came from the pumpkin patch. Isn't Mom magic? —JI

breakfast sweets & breads

129

Anne Waterman-Tanner
Irvine, California

Aunt Annie's
Cinnamon Rolls

Makes 8 cinnamon rolls

Dough
1/4 cup water
1/2 cup milk
2 tablespoons butter
1/4 cup sugar
1/2 teaspoon salt
2 1/2 cups all-purpose
   flour, divided
1 (0.25-ounce) package
   fast-acting yeast

Filling
1/2 cup packed brown sugar
1 tablespoon ground
   cinnamon
3 tablespoons butter, softened

Frosting
4 ounces cream
   cheese, softened
1/4 cup butter, softened
1 teaspoon vanilla extract
1 to 2 cups confectioners'
   sugar

To make the dough, combine the water, milk, and butter in a glass measuring cup. Microwave for a few seconds until warm (120°F to 130°F), stirring until the butter melts. In a large bowl, combine the sugar, salt, 1/2 cup of the flour, and the yeast. Add the milk mixture to the dry ingredients and mix well. Add the remaining flour 1/2 cup at a time, stirring until the dough feels stiff. (All the flour may not be needed at this point.) Knead the dough on a floured surface for 8 to 10 minutes, adding extra flour if necessary. The dough should be firm and tacky but not sticky. Cover and let rest for 10 minutes.

Roll out the dough into a rectangle about 12 by 16 inches and about 1/4 inch thick. To make the filling, combine the brown sugar and cinnamon in a bowl. Spread the softened butter or

margarine over the surface of the dough, then sprinkle with the cinnamon sugar. Working carefully from the 16-inch side, roll up the dough somewhat tightly. Cut the dough into 8 equal slices 1 1/2 to 2 inches thick. Place into a lightly greased 7 by 11-inch baking dish, evenly spaced. Cover and let rise in a warm, draft-free place for 30 minutes.

Preheat the oven to 350°F. Bake for 20 to 25 minutes, until lightly golden brown on top. While the rolls bake, make the frosting by beating the cream cheese and butter with a mixer on medium speed until light and fluffy. Add the vanilla and 1 cup of the confectioners' sugar. Beat again until well combined, taste, and add more sugar for a sweeter frosting.

When the rolls come out of the oven, slather with a generous amount of frosting. If the rolls will not be eaten all at once, frost only as needed. Leftover rolls may be frozen in individual bags and reheated in the microwave for 45 seconds before frosting. ■

My niece and myself suffer from severe nut allergies, so I developed this recipe to be safe for us to enjoy without sacrificing any of the taste, flavor, or appeal of store-bought cinnamon rolls. I created it to yield only 8 rolls—enough for guests to enjoy, or for you to make for yourself and freeze a few for later. —AWT

Karen McMillen
Redmond, Washington

Top Hat Coffee Cake

Makes 12 servings

Filling/Topping

2/3 cup packed light
  brown sugar
1 cup chopped pecans
  or walnuts
2 tablespoons butter, melted
1 teaspoon ground
  cinnamon

Cake

1/2 cup butter, softened
1 cup sugar
2 eggs
1 cup sour cream (or 2
  teaspoons vinegar plus
  milk to make 1 cup)
1 teaspoon vanilla extract
2 cups all-purpose flour
1 teaspoon baking powder
1 teaspoon baking soda
1/2 teaspoon salt

Preheat the oven to 350°F. Grease well a 9 by 13-inch baking dish.

To prepare the topping/filling, mix together all the ingredients. To make the cake, cream together the butter and sugar in a large bowl until light and fluffy. Add the eggs, sour cream, and vanilla and beat well. In a separate bowl, sift together the flour, baking powder, baking soda, and salt. Stir the dry ingredients into the creamed mixture, blending well.

Spoon half of the cake mixture into the prepared pan. Sprinkle half of the reserved filling/topping mixture over the batter. Spoon on the remaining batter, then finish with the remaining filling/topping. Bake for about 35 minutes, or until a toothpick inserted in the center comes out clean. ■

When I was growing up in western Pennsylvania in the 1940s through the '50s, dessert was reserved for very special occasions. Our favorite was this coffee cake. While it was baking, the wonderful aroma filled our little brick house. We all tried to get the piece with the most cinnamon, sugar, and nuts, and the lucky one had to guard her serving! The original recipe used a 9-inch square pan, but we use a larger pan now for more servings. —KM

Karen Peterson
Suamico, Wisconsin

Grandma Marie's
Rhubarb Kuchen

Makes 6 servings

Crust

1 1/4 cups all-purpose flour
1 tablespoon sugar
1/2 teaspoon salt
1 teaspoon baking powder
1/2 cup butter, softened
1 egg, beaten
2 tablespoons milk

Filling

3 cups (1/2-inch)
   diced rhubarb
1 (3-ounce) box strawberry-
   flavored gelatin (or
   cherry or raspberry)

Topping

1/2 cup all-purpose flour
1 cup sugar
1/4 cup butter, melted

Ice cream or whipped
   cream, for serving

Preheat the oven to 350°F. Grease a 7 by 11-inch pan.

To make the crust, mix together the flour, sugar, salt, and baking powder in a large bowl. Add the butter and mix until a fine crumbly mixture forms. Add the egg and milk and mix well. The dough should be fairly sticky, and you may have to add a bit more milk so it's not dry or crumbly. Pat the mixture into the prepared pan and bring it slightly up the sides of the pan.

To make the filling, spread out the rhubarb over the unbaked crust. Sprinkle with the gelatin powder. To make the topping, mix the flour, sugar, and butter until moistened and crumbly. Sprinkle over the rhubarb. Bake for 40 to 45 minutes, until the top is a nice golden brown and the rhubarb is bubbly. Serve warm with a scoop of ice cream or whipped cream. ■

My husband's grandmother gave us this recipe. She was a wonderful cook and baker and had many favorite recipes that were passed down to her daughter, Shirley (my mother-in-law), and then to us daughters-in-law. I have also made this with half rhubarb and half strawberries (fresh or frozen). If using frozen, let thaw a bit and drain off some of the liquid. —KP

CarolAnn Williams
Glendora, California

Nana Banana

Makes 8 servings

1 medium very ripe banana
1 tablespoon orange
    liqueur, such as Grand
    Marnier, or another
    favorite liqueur, or 1/2
    teaspoon vanilla extract

Pinch of ground cinnamon
1 (8-count) package
    refrigerated croissants
Confectioners' sugar,
    for sprinkling
Chocolate syrup, for garnish

Preheat the oven according to the croissant package directions.

Mash the ripened banana with the orange liqueur and cinnamon. Unroll the croissants and place a spoonful of the banana mixture in the middle. Roll them up and bake according to package instructions. When golden brown, place the croissants on a plate, sprinkle some confectioners' sugar on top, and drizzle some chocolate syrup over the top. ■

This was a trial quickie dessert I made from things I had on hand when my grandson wanted something sweet to eat after a Christmas party. We have tried it since with other liqueurs and vanilla extract. It is so easy and quick that I have even taken the ingredients to a friend's home and cooked it there. It was enjoyed by all! —CW

Heidi Woodruff
Coos Bay, Oregon

Cranberry and White Chocolate Scones

Makes 8 scones

1 3/4 cups all-purpose flour
1/4 cup sugar
2 1/2 teaspoons
baking powder
1/2 teaspoon salt
5 tablespoons cold
unsalted butter, cubed

6 tablespoons half-and-half
or heavy whipping cream
1 egg, beaten
1/2 cup cranberries
(fresh, frozen, or dried,
such as Craisins)
1/2 cup white
chocolate chips

Preheat the oven to 400°F. Spray a baking sheet with nonstick cooking spray. In a large bowl, blend the flour, sugar, baking powder, and salt. Cut in the butter until the mixture is crumbly. Stir in the half-and-half, egg, cranberries, and white chocolate chips until the dough begins to hold together. Turn out onto a lightly floured board and knead for about 2 minutes. Pat into a 1/2-inch-thick round, then cut into 8 wedges. Transfer to the prepared pan and bake for 14 minutes, or until golden brown. Serve hot. ■

Our weather produces some of the best-tasting cranberries. I use them in muffins, cookies, scones, breads, and sauce, and I also dry them for baking. You can substitute Craisins in any recipe that calls for raisins. —HW

breakfast sweets & breads

Delores DeVictoria
Antioch, California

Doughnut Holes

Makes 24 doughnut holes

1 cup sugar
1 cup milk
2 eggs, well beaten
2 teaspoons baking powder
Pinch of salt
1/2 teaspoon ground
  nutmeg

All-purpose flour, as needed
1 tablespoon vegetable oil, or
  more as needed, for frying
1 cup sugar mixed with
  1 teaspoon ground
  cinnamon, for sprinkling

In a large bowl, mix the sugar, milk, eggs, baking powder, salt, and nutmeg. Add flour until the consistency is between that of a batter and a dough.

Heat the oil in a skillet over medium-high heat. Spoon about 1 teaspoon of the dough into the preheated oil and fry until golden brown. Drain on a paper towel. Repeat with the remaining batter. Place the cinnamon sugar in a paper bag. Place the doughnut holes in the bag a few at a time, fold the top, and shake to coat. ■

This recipe was handed down in my husband's family as part of a poem. Once you learn the poem, you never have to rely on a recipe card again: "Cup of sugar / Cup of milk / Two eggs beat, fine as silk / Baking powder, teaspoons two / A pinch of salt, and nutmeg will do." —DD

Sheri Olson
Coburg, Oregon

Nana O's
Banana Bread

Makes 2 loaves

1 cup butter, softened

1 1/2 cups sugar

8 ounces fat-free
  peach yogurt

5 medium ripe
  bananas, mashed

1/2 teaspoon salt

1 teaspoon baking soda

4 cups all-purpose flour

1 cup chopped nuts (such
  as pecans or walnuts)

1 cup dried cranberries

Preheat the oven to 325°F. Grease or spray two standard-size loaf pans.

In a large bowl, cream the butter and sugar. Add the yogurt and bananas and mix well. Stir in the salt, baking soda, flour, nuts, and cranberries. Divide the batter between the two pans. Bake for about 1 hour and 10 minutes, or until a toothpick inserted in the center comes out clean. ■

Banana bread is one of my husband's favorites. The original recipe came from Nana O. I tweaked it a little by adding the yogurt instead of buttermilk and decreasing the sugar by 1/2 cup. If you use very ripe (black) bananas, they have more moisture than less ripe bananas, so decrease the amount of flour a bit. —SO

breakfast sweets & breads

Life is like an ice-cream
cone, you have to lick it
one day at a time.

—Charles M. Schulz

Ice Creams
& Puddings

Elaine Bellamy
Fort Cobb, Oklahoma

Berry Frozen Yogurt

Makes 6 servings

1 (32-ounce) carton low-
    fat Greek yogurt
1/2 cup nonfat
    whipping cream
1/4 to 1/2 cup sugar, to taste

2 tablespoons agave nectar
    or light corn syrup
1/2 teaspoon vanilla extract
3/4 cup berries, lightly
    sugared (I like a mix
    of different berries)

Place the yogurt in a few layers of cheesecloth and let it strain over a bowl for 2 to 4 hours in the refrigerator. Combine the strained yogurt with the whipping cream, sugar, and agave nectar. Beat until smooth. Cover and refrigerate for at least 4 hours or up to overnight. The mixture will freeze better if well chilled.

Follow your ice-cream-maker manufacturer's instructions carefully to freeze the yogurt. While frozen yogurt can be more difficult to firm up because of the low fat content, the results are delicious. About 5 minutes before it is done, add the vanilla and berries. Transfer the finished frozen yogurt to an airtight container and place in the freezer to finish firming and ripening, at least 2 hours. ■

I love low-fat tart frozen yogurt but don't like having to drive fifty miles to the closest yogurt shop. I bought a tabletop ice-cream maker and, unable to find a recipe I liked, I experimented until I came up with this.

When I was little, my grandparents were really into health food, including making their own yogurt. I didn't like it then, but years later it has become one of my staple ingredients. I sure wish I could serve my grandpa my homemade frozen yogurt. —EB

Diane Disbrow
Collinsville, Illinois

Grilled Pineapple Sundaes

Makes 5 servings

1/3 cup pure maple syrup
1/4 teaspoon ground
  cinnamon
1 (20-ounce) can pineapple
  slices in juice, drained

1/2 cup sweetened
  shredded coconut
5 scoops vanilla ice cream

Line a grill pan with nonstick aluminum foil and preheat over medium-high heat.

In a small bowl, combine the maple syrup and cinnamon. Dip each pineapple slice into the mixture and place on the grill pan. Grill over medium-high heat for 2 to 5 minutes on each side, until golden brown, basting with any leftover syrup mixture. Place the coconut in a glass pie plate and microwave on high power for 2 minutes, stirring every 30 seconds so it doesn't burn. Let cool completely to dry.

Place the ice cream scoops in individual serving dishes. Cut the pineapple slices into quarters. Top each ice cream scoop with 2 cut-up pineapple slices (8 pieces) and 1 to 2 tablespoons of toasted coconut. Serve immediately. ■

This is a quick and easy dessert that will take your taste buds to the shores of Hawaii. Aloha! —DD

Alysmay Quinton
Reno, Nevada

Yum-Yum Raspberry Christmas Pudding

Makes 8 servings

1 (3-ounce) box raspberry-flavored gelatin
1 (3-ounce) box cook-and-serve (not instant) vanilla pudding mix
2 1/2 cups water

2 cups fresh or frozen raspberries
1 envelope whipped topping mix, such as Dream Whip
1/2 cup milk
4 ounces cream cheese, softened

In a large saucepan, combine the gelatin and pudding mix with the water and cook until boiling, stirring constantly. Remove from the heat and stir in the raspberries. Refrigerate until set. It will not be as stiff as prepared gelatin.

Combine the whipped topping mix with the milk and whip according to package directions. Add the cream cheese and blend, then add the raspberry mixture and blend well. Refrigerate for at least 1 hour, or until set. Serve cold, and refrigerate leftovers. ■

My mother-in-law, Dorothy Quinton, liked to make Jell-O salads and was always creating her own recipes. She gave me this recipe more than thirty-five years ago at Christmastime. My children thought it was yummy, so they started calling it "Yum-Yum." To this day, they ask if I'm making "Yum-Yum" for Thanksgiving and Christmas dinner. —AQ

ice creams & puddings

145

H. Joyce Kelley
Taylorville, Illinois

Angel Pudding

Makes 24 servings

1 (0.25-ounce) envelope
  unflavored gelatin
1/4 cup cold water
1/2 cup boiling water
3/4 cup sugar

1 cup orange juice
Juice of 1/2 lemon
2 cups heavy
  whipping cream
1 prepared angel food cake

In a small bowl, soak the gelatin in the cold water; let stand for 5 minutes. In a separate bowl, combine the boiling water, sugar, orange juice, and lemon juice. Stir in the gelatin mixture, then refrigerate while you whip the cream.

In a large bowl with a mixer, whip the cream first on low speed, then increase the speed a bit until thickened. Add the gelatin mixture and mix well. Chill completely. Remove any brown spots from the cake. Cut the cake into bite-size pieces and layer the pieces and the cream mixture in a 9 by 13-inch baking dish. Refrigerate for 12 hours before serving. ■

My mother was born in Dortmund, Germany, and lived to the age of ninety-eight. This is a family recipe she used to make around the holidays. It is a very light dessert. Our family still makes it. —HJK

Kim Guidry
Perry, Georgia

Old-Fashioned
"Boo-Yee"

Makes 8 servings

8 cups milk
1 1/4 cups sugar
2/3 cup cornstarch
2 eggs
1/2 cup butter (not
　margarine)
1 teaspoon vanilla extract

1 teaspoon butter or
　nut flavoring (or 1
　teaspoon more vanilla)
1 (5-ounce) can
　evaporated milk
Angel food or white
　cake, for serving

Place the milk in a large saucepan over medium heat. In a small bowl, whisk together the sugar and cornstarch. Add the eggs and whisk. Add this mixture to the milk. Cook, stirring constantly so the bottom does not stick, until thick. (It may still stick some.) When thick, stir in the butter. When the butter has melted, add the extract and flavoring. Remove from the heat and start beating with a mixer on medium-low speed. Slowly add the evaporated milk and continue beating until smooth. Serve over pieces of angel food cake or white cake. ■

My husband is from about as far south as you can
go in Louisiana, and he grew up cooking the usual
Cajun dishes such as jambalaya, étouffée, and gumbo.
He learned at a young age by cooking for his father
and his father's crew on a shrimp boat. I love all the
Cajun main dishes, but I also love the sweets, including
pralines and custards, and this recipe, which was
given to me by one of my husband's aunts. —KG

ice creams & puddings

147

Mirella Baltazar
Duarte, California

Mery's Flan

Makes 1 Bundt-size flan

2 (12-ounce) cans
    evaporated milk
2 (14-ounce) cans sweetened
    condensed milk

4 eggs
1 tablespoon vanilla extract
1 cup sugar

Preheat the oven to 500°F.

In a large bowl, mix together both milks, the eggs, and the vanilla. Place the sugar in a metal Bundt pan and place the pan on top of the stove over medium heat to caramelize until light brown. Watch carefully.

Pour the milk mixture on top of the sugar and do not stir. Place the Bundt pan in a roasting pan and add water to the roasting pan until it is halfway up the side of the Bundt pan. Bake for 1 hour to 1 hour and 15 minutes, until a toothpick inserted into the center comes out clean. Remove from the roasting pan and while it's still hot, very carefully move the pan in a circular motion until you see the flan separate from the pan. Carefully invert the hot flan onto a serving plate. The caramelized sugar should drip all around the flan. Refrigerate any leftovers. ■

I am from Peru, in South America, and my mother always used to make this flan for every party, ever since I was a little girl. —MB

Kama Massmann
Fairview, Texas

Flan

Makes 1 flan

1 (14-ounce) can sweetened
  condensed milk
1 (12-ounce) can
  evaporated milk

5 eggs
1 tablespoon vanilla extract
1/4 cup sugar

Preheat the oven to 350°F. In a large bowl, beat the sweetened condensed milk, evaporated milk, eggs, and vanilla until just blended.

Place the sugar in a metal flanera pan (or Bundt pan) on the stovetop over medium heat and cook until caramelized. Watch carefully. Pour the milk mixture on top of the caramelized sugar and cover with aluminum foil. Place the pan in a roasting pan, fill it with water to come halfway up the side of the flan pan, and bake for about 1 hour and 30 minutes, or until set. Remove from the roasting pan and let stand until completely cool before inverting onto a serving dish. Refrigerate any leftovers. ■

I got this recipe from my pastor's wife while living in Mexico doing mission work. It's amazing, and everyone loves it! —KM

ice creams & puddings

Seize the moment. Remember all those women on the *Titanic* who waved off the dessert cart.

—Erma Bombeck

Miscellaneous

Cindy Chatleain
Mankato, Minnesota

Cookie Spa Treatmint

Makes one 9 by 13-inch pie

32 crème-filled chocolate sandwich cookies (such as Oreos), finely crushed

2 cups heavy whipping cream

1 tablespoon sugar, or as desired

1/2 teaspoon vanilla extract, or as desired

1 cup pastel pillow mints

2 cups mini pastel marshmallows

Grease a 9 by 13-inch baking dish. Place half of the crushed cookies in the pan.

In a large bowl with a mixer, whip the heavy whipping cream. Gradually add a little sugar and vanilla to suit your taste. Use a spatula to fold in the pillow mints and the marshmallows. Spread the mixture over the crushed cookies. Top with the remaining crushed cookies. Refrigerate for 2 days before serving. ■

My mom made this for holidays when I was growing up. She loved the way it looked at Christmas and Easter. I remember separating the pastel mints and marshmallows at Christmas so it was just the green, pink, and white ones. I think she just wanted to keep me busy. After a big meal, this will make your tummy feel like it went to the spa. —CC

Julie Webb
Easton, Maryland

Heavenly Chocolate Cookie Cloud

Makes 12 servings

1 (1-pound) package
crème-filled chocolate
sandwich cookies (such
as Oreos), crushed

1 cup butter, melted

1 (8-ounce) package
cream cheese, softened

2 (8-ounce) containers
frozen whipped
topping, thawed

1 cup confectioners' sugar

1 (4.6-ounce) box instant
chocolate pudding mix

3 cups milk

Set aside 3/4 cup of the crushed cookies. Spread the remaining crushed cookies evenly across the bottom of a 9 by 13-inch baking pan. Pour the melted butter over the cookies. Refrigerate while you prepare the next layer.

In a large bowl with a mixer, beat the cream cheese, one container of the whipped topping, and the confectioners' sugar on medium speed until smooth. Spread the mixture over the cookie layer and return the pan to the refrigerator.

In a large bowl, combine the pudding mix and milk according to the package directions. Spread the pudding layer over the cream cheese layer. Top with remaining container of whipped topping and sprinkle with the reserved crushed cookies. Refrigerate for at least 1 hour before serving. ■

Easy and delicious, this is the most-requested birthday dessert in our house . . . and with seven kids, we get to enjoy it often! —JW

miscellaneous

153

Kimlee Bublitz
Newbury Park, California

Grasshopper Soufflé

Makes 10 servings

1 (0.25-ounce) envelope
  unflavored gelatin
1/2 cup water
1/4 cup sugar
1/8 teaspoon salt
3 egg yolks, beaten
1/4 cup crème de
  menthe liqueur
1/4 cup crème de
  cacao liqueur
1 cup heavy whipping cream
3 egg whites, beaten
  until frothy
1/4 cup confectioners' sugar
2 tablespoons finely chopped
  pistachios, for garnish

In a medium saucepan over low heat, combine the gelatin and water. Once the gelatin softens, add the sugar and stir well. Add the salt and egg yolks. Cook over low heat, stirring, until slightly thickened. Add both liqueurs and stir well. Pour the mixture into a deep bowl and refrigerate for 20 minutes, or until the mixture thickens.

In a medium bowl with a mixer, beat the whipping cream on high speed until almost stiff, and then add the egg whites and confectioners' sugar. When stiff peaks have formed, fold the mixture into the chilled soufflé mixture. Pour the soufflé into a glass bowl or large springform pan. Chill for at least 1 hour. If using a springform pan, gently run a warm knife around the edges and carefully unmold. Garnish the top with the pistachios. ■

This yummy dish was one of the first dishes I cooked in home ec at Brookfield Central High School, Brookfield, Wisconsin. You don't hear about grasshoppers anymore—it must have been the times of the late 1960s. It's still a hit at my parties and a hoot to serve to my old friends who remember those days. This goes down so smooth, with just a hint of liqueur. —KB

Pat Waters
St. Louis, Missouri

Éclair Ring

Makes 8 to 12 servings

Shell

1 cup water
1/2 cup butter or margarine
1 cup all-purpose flour
1/4 teaspoon salt
4 eggs

Filling

2 (3.4-ounce) boxes instant
  vanilla pudding mix
2 cups milk
1 cup heavy whipping cream
1/4 cup sugar
1 teaspoon vanilla extract

Frosting

1 tablespoon butter
2 tablespoons unsweetened
  cocoa powder
1 1/2 cups confectioners'
  sugar, sifted
2 tablespoons milk
1 teaspoon vanilla extract

To make the shell, preheat the oven to 400°F. In a medium saucepan over medium heat, bring the water and butter to a boil and then decrease the heat to low. Add the flour and salt and stir to form a ball. Remove from the heat and beat in the eggs, one at a time. Shape into a 7-inch circle on an ungreased baking sheet. Bake for 40 minutes, turn off the oven, and leave it in the oven for an additional 15 minutes. Let cool completely, then split through the middle to form a top and bottom.

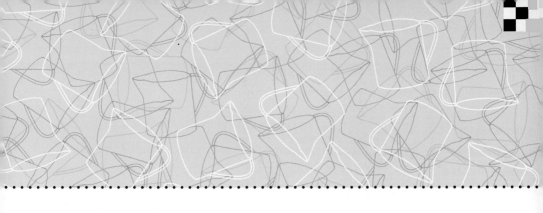

To make the filling, combine the pudding mix and milk in a medium bowl. Beat with a mixer for 2 minutes on medium-low speed, then refrigerate for 30 minutes. In a separate bowl, on medium speed, whip the heavy cream, sugar, and vanilla until fluffy. Fold the cream into the pudding mixture and refrigerate.

To make the frosting, melt the butter in a medium saucepan over medium-low heat and stir in the cocoa powder. Slowly add the confectioners' sugar, milk, and vanilla and stir until smooth. To assemble the éclair, spoon the filling onto the bottom half of the shell, place the top half of the shell over the filling, then pour the frosting over the top. ■

I learned of this treat in 1986 while living in New Hampshire. I don't consider myself much of a cook, but maybe a bit of a baker! —PW

miscellaneous

Betsy Hada
El Sobrante, California

Sweet Potato Streusel Casserole

Makes 12 servings

5 pounds large
  sweet potatoes
1/2 cup butter, cut into
  pieces, softened
Zest and juice of 1
  large orange
2 tablespoons grated
  fresh ginger
1/2 teaspoon ground
  cardamom
1/2 teaspoon ground mace
2 teaspoons salt
1 teaspoon ground
  black pepper
3 eggs, beaten

Topping
1 cup all-purpose flour
2/3 cup packed brown sugar
1/2 cup cold butter, cubed
1 cup old-fashioned
  rolled oats
2/3 cup chopped
  pecans (optional)

Preheat the oven to 375°F. Bake the sweet potatoes until you can pierce them with a fork, at least 1 hour. Let cool until you can take off the skins (they should still be fairly warm). Mash with a hand masher. Add the butter and mash until melted in. Then add the orange zest and juice, ginger, cardamom, mace, salt, and pepper. Mix with the potato masher. Use a spatula to mix in the eggs. Transfer the mixture to a deep 10 by 13-inch casserole dish, leaving at least 1 inch for the topping. Decrease the oven temperature to 350°F.

To make the topping, mix the flour and brown sugar in a medium bowl. Blend in the butter with a pastry blender, two knives, or your fingers. Add the oats and pecans. Squeeze the mixture into handfuls so it clumps up as you spread it onto the sweet potato mixture. (This leaves crunchier parts rather than uniform crumbles. At this point, you may refrigerate overnight or longer before baking.)

Bake for about 1 hour or until the topping browns and the center is fully warmed. If you refrigerated the casserole overnight, it will take about 15 minutes longer to bake. ■

One Thanksgiving, twenty years or more ago, I was tired of the same old sweet potato recipes, so I tinkered with a little of this and a little of that until I had made up this recipe. My sister-in-law immediately decreed that I needed to bring it every year. Each year it changed slightly, and I didn't take notes. Finally, one year (at the behest of another relative), I carefully took note of everything and wrote up the recipe. —BH

miscellaneous

Victoria Grusing
Newport, Oregon

Cranberry Relish

Makes 10 servings

1 cup water
1 (12-ounce) bag fresh
   or frozen cranberries

1 (8-ounce) jar orange
   marmalade

Bring the water to a boil. Add the cranberries and return to a boil. Cook, stirring, until the berries begin to burst. Remove from the heat and stir in the marmalade. ∎

My dearest friend found and tried this recipe and took a family from being one not liking cranberries to being one that happily uses this relish on rolls. It is too easy, so it must be shared. —VG

Mary Jo Caliendo
Pittsburgh, Pennsylvania

Cranberry Salad Delight

Makes 12 servings

1 (12-ounce) bag
  fresh cranberries
1 cup diced apples
1 cup seedless grape halves
1 cup sugar

1 cup chopped walnuts
1 cup water
3 cups mini marshmallows
1 1/2 cups frozen whipped
  topping, thawed

Place the cranberries in a blender and crush them. Transfer them to a large bowl and add the apples, grape halves, sugar, walnuts, and water. Stir. Cover the bowl and refrigerate overnight.

Add the marshmallows and whipped topping to the chilled ingredients and gently mix everything together. Transfer the mixture to a large glass serving bowl and chill until ready to eat. ■

This is so delicious and easy to make. The recipe was a family favorite that my great-aunt prepared every year for Thanksgiving and Christmas dinner. We all looked forward to eating it with our turkey. —MC

miscellaneous

Shawnnita Fairbairn
Moranbah, Australia

Pretzel Salad

Makes 12 servings

Crust
3/4 cup butter, melted
3 tablespoons sugar
2/3 cups broken bow-
  shaped pretzels

Filling
2 (8-ounce) packages
  cream cheese, softened
1 cup sugar
1/2 cup heavy
  whipping cream

Topping
1 (3-ounce) box strawberry-
  flavored gelatin
1 cup boiling water
1 cup cold water
13 ounces frozen
  strawberries or 1 pint
  fresh, halved lengthwise

Preheat the oven to 350°F. Grease a 9 by 13-inch baking dish. To make the crust, combine the butter and sugar in a medium bowl and mix well. Stir in the pretzels. Pat into the prepared pan. Bake for 8 to 10 minutes, until lightly golden. Set on a wire rack to cool completely.

To make the filling, combine the cream cheese and sugar in a large bowl and mix really well. Mix in the whipping cream. Spread over the cooled crust, cover with plastic wrap, and chill while you make the topping.

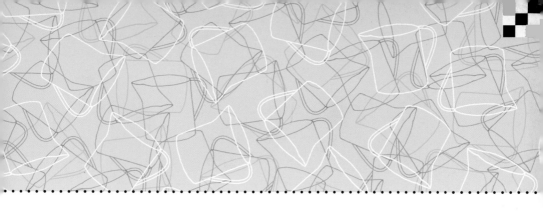

Dissolve the strawberry gelatin in the boiling water. Add the cold water and refrigerate for 15 to 20 minutes, covered, but don't allow it to turn solid. Once the gelatin mixture has cooled, remove it and the filled crust from the refrigerator. While holding a spoon to break the flow, slowly pour the gelatin mixture all over the filling. (The spoon will prevent the stream of gelatin from making divots in the still-soft filling.) Gently push the halved strawberries through the gelatin and down into the filling a bit so they don't float. Refrigerate for at least 6 hours, but it's best if refrigerated overnight. ■

This lovely, sweet-and-salty dessert has been handed down through three generations from my grandmother Jessie Sutherland to my mother, Anita Gardner, to me. The recipe is affectionately stained, brown with age, and a little tattered. It's soothed broken hearts in our home of four boys and helped us celebrate many milestones and holidays. I'm looking forward to passing it down to my sons and daughters-in-law. —SF

miscellaneous

Vicky Denning
Apopka, Florida

Frog Eye Salad

Makes 8 to 10 servings

3/4 cup sugar
1 tablespoon all-purpose flour
1/2 teaspoon salt
2/3 cup pineapple juice
1 egg, beaten
1 tablespoon freshly
squeezed lemon juice
1 (8-ounce) package
acini di pepe pasta,
cooked according to
package directions

2 (11-ounce) cans mandarin
oranges, drained
1 (20-ounce) can crushed
pineapple, drained
1 (8-ounce) can diced
pineapple, drained
1 cup mini marshmallows
1 (8-ounce) container frozen
whipped topping, thawed

In a small saucepan over medium heat, mix the sugar, flour, salt, pineapple juice, and egg. Cook, stirring constantly, until thickened. Add the lemon juice and remove from the heat to cool. Stir in the cooked pasta. Cover and chill overnight. Combine the remaining ingredients and stir into the pasta mixture. Chill for 1 hour before serving. The salad will keep for 1 week in the refrigerator in a tightly sealed container. Do not freeze. ■

I have four children and twelve grandchildren, and I like to serve this for family get-togethers. They all love it, but my oldest grandson wouldn't eat it for a long time, and when he finally told me why, it was, "Nana, I just can't eat frog's eyes." I also take it to church suppers, where it is always a big hit. —VD

Kimberly Edwards
Sallisaw, Oklahoma

Grandma Wanzer's
Holiday Dessert

Makes 10 servings

1 (3-ounce) box strawberry-
flavored gelatin (or
your favorite flavor)
1 (8-ounce) container frozen
whipped topping, thawed
1 (8-ounce) can crushed
pineapple, drained

1/2 (10-ounce) jar
maraschino cherries,
drained and chopped
(optional)
1 (16-ounce) container
small-curd cottage cheese
1/4 cup chopped nuts
(such as pecans or
walnuts; optional)

Stir together all of the ingredients in a medium bowl. Cover
and refrigerate for 2 hours to firm up before serving. ■

A day or so before Easter one year, I was preparing
this dessert when my older brother (who was almost fifty)
dropped by. He asked what I was making, so I told him
"Grandma's Dessert," and he asked why I was putting
cottage cheese in it (he *hates* cottage cheese). I told him
that Grandma had *always* put cottage cheese in it, and we
got into a spat about it until I showed him Grandma's old
recipe card with her writing. He stopped arguing, but he
also stopped eating that dessert. Brothers! No matter how
old they get, they can still act just like little kids! —KE

miscellaneous

Glenda Jacobs
Norwalk, California

"I'm in the Mood for More"
Fruit Salad

Makes 7 servings

2 (15-ounce) cans fruit
 cocktail, drained
1 (20-ounce) can crushed
 pineapple, drained
1 (8-ounce) container
 sour cream
1 (4-ounce) bag
 chopped pecans

2 medium bananas,
 ripe to perfection
Sweetened shredded
 coconut (optional)
Mini marshmallows
 (optional)

In a large bowl, combine the fruit cocktail and crushed pineapple. Stir in half the container of sour cream. Taste and add more sour cream as desired. The consistency should be creamy, not runny. Do the same with the pecans: Stir in half, then add more to taste. Slice in the bananas, stirring as you go along. (The remaining few slices can top the salad for visual effect.) If you wish, stir in some coconut and mini marshmallows. This salad should be served immediately, before the bananas turn brown. It does not keep well for leftovers, but there is usually no problem with finishing it at serving time! ■

I was first introduced to this salad in my twenties, and when I saw my friend fold in the sour cream I almost refused it. But I tried it, and it was delicious. Now when I make it, I hear, "I'm in the mood for more," and I say, "Sorry—it's all gone!" Until next time. —GJ

Anna Morgan
Grand Blanc, Michigan

Grilled Peach Dessert

Makes 8 servings

4 large peaches, peeled, halved, and pitted
1/4 cup packed brown sugar

2 tablespoons ground cinnamon
8 large marshmallows
Vanilla ice cream, for serving

Prepare a medium-hot grill. Spray a 9 by 13-inch baking pan with nonstick cooking spray. Slice a small piece off the back of each peach half to help it stay level in the pan. Place each peach half in the pan, pitted side up. Sprinkle with the brown sugar and then the cinnamon. Place a marshmallow on top of each, nestled where the pit used to be.

Place the peaches on the grill grate, close the lid, and grill for about 20 minutes, or until bubbly and the marshmallows are golden brown. Serve with vanilla ice cream. ■

I am a Weber grill enthusiast, and I believe you can cook anything on one. My mother used to make this recipe from an old Weber cookbook (circa 1970s). She received a Weber grill (with the book) as a gift from her employer. The grill was a limited-edition red, and I was in awe. When I grill this dessert, it reminds me of those days and my mother. —AM

miscellaneous

Linda Shickell
Nevada, Iowa

Cherry Tortilla Dessert

Makes 10 servings

1 cup sugar
1/2 cup water
1/2 cup butter
10 small flour tortillas
Ground cinnamon,
   for sprinkling

1 (21-ounce) can
   cherry pie filling
Frozen whipped
   topping, thawed, or
   vanilla ice cream, for
   serving (optional)

Grease a 9 by 13-inch baking dish. Combine the sugar, water, and butter in a medium saucepan over medium heat and bring to a rolling boil. Sprinkle each tortilla with cinnamon. Place about 2 1/2 tablespoons of pie filling in the middle of each tortilla. Roll up each tortilla and place seam side down in the prepared pan. Pour the boiling mixture over the tortillas. Sprinkle with more cinnamon. Let rest for 40 minutes.

Preheat the oven to 350°F. Bake for 25 minutes, or until brown and crispy. Serve warm with warm syrup from the baking dish spooned over each tortilla. You may serve it with whipped topping or ice cream as well. ∎

This recipe was given to me several years ago by a friend, and I especially like to serve it each Christmas when I have friends and neighbors in for coffee. I receive many compliments on it, as it is something a little different, and the prep time is minimal for such a pretty and tasty dessert. —LS

Cynthia Cooke
Torrance, California

Christmas Cereal

Makes 8 cups

6 cups Crispix cereal

2 cups pecans

1/2 cup butter

3/4 cup packed brown sugar

Preheat the oven to 350°F. Place the cereal and pecans in a deep baking pan. In a medium saucepan, melt the butter over low heat. Add the brown sugar, increase the heat slightly, and cook until the bubbles are thick and large. Drizzle the mixture over the cereal and pecans. Toss gently with a spatula to coat. Bake for about 4 minutes. Toss, then bake for another 4 minutes. Let cool. ■

I give this every year to the people I work with.
I place it in cute, clear gift bags sealed with a
twist tie, or in decorative tins or containers. The
comments you get will amaze you! —CC

miscellaneous

Metric Conversions & Equivalents

Approximate Metric Equivalents

Volume

1/4 teaspoon = 1 milliliter

1/2 teaspoon = 2.5 milliliters

3/4 teaspoon = 4 milliliters

1 teaspoon = 5 milliliters

1 1/4 teaspoons = 6 milliliters

1 1/2 teaspoons = 7.5 milliliters

1 3/4 teaspoons = 8.5 milliliters

2 teaspoons = 10 milliliters

1 tablespoon (1/2 fluid ounce) = 15 milliliters

2 tablespoons (1 fluid ounce) = 30 milliliters

1/4 cup = 60 milliliters

1/3 cup = 80 milliliters

1/2 cup (4 fluid ounces) = 120 milliliters

2/3 cup = 160 milliliters

3/4 cup = 180 milliliters

1 cup (8 fluid ounces) = 240 milliliters

1 1/4 cups = 300 milliliters

1 1/2 cups (12 fluid ounces) = 360 milliliters

1 2/3 cups = 400 milliliters

2 cups (1 pint) = 460 milliliters

3 cups = 700 milliliters

4 cups (1 quart) = 0.95 liter

1 quart plus 1/4 cup = 1 liter

4 quarts (1 gallon) = 3.8 liters

Length

1/8 inch = 3 millimeters

1/4 inch = 6 millimeters

1/2 inch = 1.25 centimeters

1 inch = 2.5 centimeters

2 inches = 5 centimeters

2 1/2 inches = 6 centimeters

4 inches = 10 centimeters

5 inches = 13 centimeters

6 inches = 15.25 centimeters

12 inches (1 foot) = 30 centimeters

Weight

1/4 ounce = 7 grams	3 ounces = 85 grams
1/2 ounce = 14 grams	4 ounces (1/4 pound) = 113 grams
3/4 ounce = 21 grams	5 ounces = 142 grams
1 ounce = 28 grams	6 ounces = 170 grams
1 1/4 ounces = 35 grams	7 ounces = 198 grams
1 1/2 ounces = 42.5 grams	8 ounces (1/2 pound) = 227 grams
1 2/3 ounces = 45 grams	16 ounces (1 pound) = 454 grams
2 ounces = 57 grams	35.25 ounces (2.2 pounds) = 1 kilogram

Metric Conversion Formulas

To Convert	Multiply
Ounces to grams	Ounces by 28.35
Pounds to kilograms	Pounds by 0.454
Teaspoons to milliliters	Teaspoons by 4.93
Tablespoons to milliliters	Tablespoons by 14.79
Fluid ounces to milliliters	Fluid ounces by 29.57
Cups to milliliters	Cups by 236.59
Cups to liters	Cups by 0.236
Pints to liters	Pints by 0.473
Quarts to liters	Quarts by 0.946
Gallons to liters	Gallons by 3.785
Inches to centimeters	Inches by 2.54

Oven Temperatures

To convert Fahrenheit to Celsius, subtract 32 from Fahrenheit, multiply the result by 5, then divide by 9.

Description	Fahrenheit	Celsius	British Gas Mark
Very cool	200°	95°	0
Very cool	225°	110°	1/4
Very cool	250°	120°	1/2
Cool	275°	135°	1
Cool	300°	150°	2
Warm	325°	165°	3
Moderate	350°	175°	4
Moderately hot	375°	190°	5
Fairly hot	400°	200°	6
Hot	425°	220°	7
Very hot	450°	230°	8
Very hot	475°	245°	9

Common Ingredients and Their Approximate Equivalents

1 cup uncooked rice = 225 grams

1 cup all-purpose flour = 140 grams

1 stick butter (4 ounces • 1/2 cup • 8 tablespoons) = 110 grams

1 cup butter (8 ounces • 2 sticks • 16 tablespoons) = 220 grams

1 cup brown sugar, firmly packed = 225 grams

1 cup granulated sugar = 200 grams

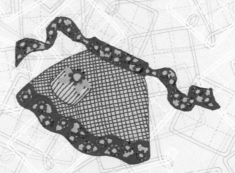

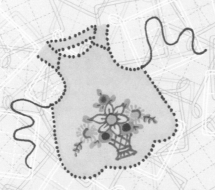

Information compiled from a variety of sources, including *Recipes into Type* by Joan Whitman and Dolores Simon (Newton, MA: Biscuit Books, 2000); *The New Food Lover's Companion* by Sharon Tyler Herbst (Hauppauge, NY: Barron's, 1995); and *Rosemary Brown's Big Kitchen Instruction Book* (Kansas City, MO: Andrews McMeel, 1998).

Index

Cookies, Bars & Brownies

Candies & Fudge